19 DAYS

Anne M. St. Clair

Published by Loumark Press

ISBN: 978-1-947635-63-0

For more information or to contact the author, please visit 19DaysBook.com

To my dearest friend Kim, whose courage and strength inspired so many.

Note to Readers

The correspondence and dialogue between the characters of this story are written in their voice. Misspellings, a combination of British and English spelling, and incorrect grammar in emails and instant messages are intentional and reflect the authenticity of the conversations. Some have been identified for the reader using (sic). Comments in italics reflect my thoughts and feelings. The days listed in the Table of Contents correspond to the days that I communicated with Tom Miller.

Table of Contents

Day 1, January 2

The Wink

Sometimes, you just need to take a leap of faith and do what feels uncomfortable to move ahead. It was January 2, and my alma mater was playing in a major bowl game. It was a great day for the Lions, but it would have been more fun to be watching the game with friends and family. I'd had no bowl invites that year.

Getting the news that my ex had become engaged over Christmas was still weighing on my emotions. Yes, I had initiated the divorce, but that didn't mean the finality of my ex marrying another woman wasn't difficult to accept.

With all the single men in the world, how was it that none of my friends knew any of them? In the four years I had been divorced, no one had ever introduced me to another man. I was dead set against being involved with someone at work. And as a consultant, dating my clients was totally out of the question.

And then there was the internet. Did I have to really put myself out there? It seemed so ridiculous. I was smart, successful, easygoing, and physically fit. Did I really have to go on a website to find a man? As the reality set in that I was not above signing up for a dating site, I began to write my profile.

I'm outgoing, optimistic, fun-loving, and love to laugh. Family and friends are important to me. I love cycling, photography, working out, and going to football, hockey, and baseball games. I'm well-traveled and lived for several years in Australia and Europe. I love how the air smells before it rains, the stillness of a snowy night, the feel of sand between my toes. I want to be the person someone thinks of as they fall asleep at night and to be the one who makes them smile when they wake.

Divorced, 5'7", slender/toned, Christian/Catholic, kids (they live on their own), non-smoking, social drinker.

With much anxiety, I clicked join and took a deep breath. Within seconds, another profile winked at me. I wasn't sure what to do with that wink. *Wow, that was fast,* I thought. And then a picture flashed up from Bestmoments40. He was good looking … shockingly handsome … and he wanted to talk to ME! OK, then; I had started the online dating process.

> **Best:** Hi, I'm Tom.
> **Annie:** Hi Tom, I'm Annie. What are you up to?
> **Best:** Are you new to the site, Annie?
> **Annie:** Is it that obvious?
> **Best:** Want to get off the site email and go onto our personal email?
> **Annie:** Sure, my email address is anniem@yahoo.com

I didn't heed the site's guidance, 'Do not communicate off the site.' Instead, I thought how easy it was to meet someone and begin talking to them. Maybe dating sites weren't so bad after all. I began to feel the anxiety lessen and thought, *I can do this.*

> **From:** Tom Miller<happysmile4868@gmail.com>
> **Sent:** Monday, January 2, 2017 10:20 PM
> **To:** anniem@yahoo.com
> **Subject:** Hello Annie
>
> It's me, Tom … Let me know whenever you get this.

> **From:** anniem@yahoo.com
> **Sent:** Monday, January 2, 2017 11:00 PM
> **To:** Tom Miller <happysmile4868@gmail.com>
> **Subject:** Re: Hello Annie
>
> Hey Tom. I received your email. What a great email address ... 'happy smile' ...

> **From:** Tom Miller <happysmile4868@gmail.com>
> **Sent:** Monday, January 2, 2017 11:13 PM
> **To:** anniem@yahoo.com
> **Subject:** Hello Annie
>
> Thank you … I enjoy talking to you and I would like us to keep this going … What are you doing now?

From: anniem@yahoo.com
Sent: Tuesday, January 2, 2017 11:23 PM
To: Tom Miller <happysmile4868@gmail.com>
Subject: Re: Hello Annie

Likewise. Just getting things ready for work after having been off for Christmas.

From: Tom Miller <happysmile4868@gmail.com>
Sent: Monday, January 2, 2017 11:39 PM
To: anniem@yahoo.com
Subject: Hello Annie

Okay, I will leave you to get your things done and get some sleep. I will email you tomorrow morning and tell you a bit about me.

From: anniem@yahoo.com
Sent: Monday, January 2, 2017 11:48 PM
To: Tom Miller <happysmile4868@gmail.com>
Subject: Re: Hello Annie

Sounds good. Talk to you then! Have a restful evening!

Day 2, January 3

Google Hangouts

From: Tom Miller <happysmile4868@gmail.com>
Sent: Tuesday, January 3, 2017 7:05 AM
To: anniem@yahoo.com
Subject: Re: Hello Annie

Good morning, Annie. What can I say about myself? Well, I'm quite simple, really. I like pretty much anything, as long as it's in good company. I like nature, sciences, literature, arts, music, movies, sports, travels, and many more (sic). I am pretty high energy and stay on the go. I'm a down to earth, independent guy. I love living life to the fullest. I enjoy dinner and a movie, dancing, taking a walk, and one-on-one time. I like eating Mexican, Thai, Chinese, sushi, and seafood. I stay in good physical condition. Being dressed up and being casual are both cool. I am serious about everything I do, including having fun. I like to use humor some (sic). I am both active and laid back. I am resourceful, creative, adventurous, expressive, organized, and practical. I am caring and sensitive with a big heart. I like commitment and honesty. I appreciate both simple and sophisticated pleasures. Two-way communication is a must.

I have come to realize over the last few years that dating at 50s (sic) is a much different ballgame to when I was younger. I am a person with a lot of positive energy, and I consider myself a very upbeat, glass-half-full type of person. I enjoy everything from a good jazz concert to a gathering with friends to watch an Arizona Cardinals or LA Rams game. I've always considered myself as a work in progress. You never stop learning, growing, and getting better. I believe in living a healthy lifestyle. Although I'm far from a muscle head, I do enjoy exercising and staying fit. To me, it is the best way to keep feeling and looking youthful.

My relationship will be with a positive and optimistic person. I am looking for someone to share fun times with. I enjoy traveling, fitness, cooking, dining out, and music. I love to make people laugh, so a great sense of humor is a must. I enjoy an independent lifestyle. I'm ideally looking for a woman with a romantic side and a sense of adventure. I'm completely open to ethnic background and race. Physically, I'm more attracted to a woman with a kind heart. I never get tired of a nice smile and a pleasant demeanor. The rest we can work on. However, I'd really like to meet someone who is compatible with me to spend time with.

I guess you can say that I'm guilty of being too career focused over the last decade to focus on a committed relationship. Someone who is caring and thoughtful, with a two-person team mentality. Not one who is materialistic and self-centered. No drama trauma. No head games! She will be both a great friend and (a) lover. Mutual chemistry and physical sexual attraction will have to exist. If you already have a boyfriend, I am not interested. I am not looking for someone just to email back and forth forever. Only those that are truly sincere and serious about meeting me for a potential relationship, please. I appreciate honesty, sincerity, truth, caring, understanding in every way.

Your new friend,

Tom

From: anniem@yahoo.com
Sent: Tuesday, January 3, 2017 7:37 AM
To: Tom Miller <happysmile4868@gmail.com>
Subject: Re: Hello Annie

Hey Tom,

Thanks for reaching out this morning. I'm on the train on my way to Philly. I'm not a big fan of typing long notes on my phone, so I'll email you back later today from my laptop. Have some meetings first thing, so maybe around lunchtime. By the way, you sound amazing! Love the photo of you at the concert.

This guy is really handsome! Dresses nice. Enjoys outdoor concerts. So far, so good.

From: Tom Miller <happysmile4868@gmail.com>
Sent: Tuesday, January 3, 2017 7:45 AM
To: anniem@yahoo.com
Subject: Re: Hello Annie

Okay. Let me know whenever you are free to talk. Take care and have a great meeting.

From: anniem@yahoo.com
Sent: Tuesday, January 3, 2017 12:32 PM
To: Tom Miller <happysmile4868@gmail.com>
Subject: Re: Hello Annie

Hi Tom,

I have never written an email like this. I must admit, it's a bit strange, but here goes.

What I want you to know about me ...

My best friend right now is my 95-(soon to be 96)-year-old mom who still lives independently in the home she and my dad built when they were married! She is an amazing woman! The oldest of nine children who grew up on a farm in the Midwest. She not only finished high school (which was a big deal back then) but also got her BA and her masters! I live about 30 minutes from her and spend most of my weekends taking her out to dinner, movies, shows, etc. In fact, my Christmas present to her was tickets to see Hamilton in NYC; she was thrilled! She's so healthy. I'm fortunate to have this time with her.

My son Jack (he's 25) is a great young man. He's still working on finding the 'career' job, but he'll find his way. He's smart as hell and so kind and considerate and a great listener. He'd make a great counselor! He'd like to work in research and analysis and get his masters. He's easygoing, creative, and my pride and joy!

I'm the youngest of four, the baby! I have two sisters and a brother. I'm close to all of them. I'm an optimist and always have been. I always have a smile on my face (unless I'm deep in thought) and love to laugh. In fact, I'm kind of known for my laugh.

I have a strong work ethic. That is something my dad instilled in me. I have worked in consulting for nearly 10 years and just love it! Before that, I was in finance and HR for a global chemical company. When I was with the chemical company, I had the opportunity to live and work overseas in Australia for three and a half years and Belgium for four years. During that time, I had the wonderful chance to travel to Asia, South America, and Eastern and Western Europe. That was a dream come true! I love to travel, explore new places, and see the world.

I treasure friendships. I think this is something especially important to women. I still have close friendships with my girlfriends from high school. There are five of us who get together for dinner every couple of months. I also still connect with a number of women from college. In fact, there is a large group of us meeting in NYC in April. And there are work friends. I have a handful of wonderful women I have worked with on consulting projects who have become good friends. I am very loyal to my friendships.

I enjoy working out, always have! I used to be a jogger and miss it tremendously, but now do weights, cycling, and the elliptical. I agree with you that working out keeps us youthful. I love shoes and boots. As you, I like to dress up, but am comfortable in stretch pants and a T-shirt.

I used to have a beagle; he was Jack's dog. But it's hard to have a dog when traveling so much for work and taking vacations, so I won't get another anytime soon. His name was Zach, and he was a pistol. Way too smart for his own good! I love the outdoors as well, particular(ly) during the spring and fall months. I enjoy hiking and camping, but I prefer to have a place with a shower and (a) toilet.

I'm pretty adventurous. I have the attitude that you 'only live once', so I like to have fun! I went skydiving once and fell in love with it! I love to zip line, quad, sled (not ski ... I'll tell you why later).

I don't 'love' to cook, but I am pretty good at it. I would rather cook with someone. I'll opt for popcorn before making a meal for myself! My most unhealthy habit is drinking Diet Coke or Diet Pepsi! Could be worse, right? I love vanilla ice cream and M&M's (not together), and rarely buy them or else I'd be enormous!

I like when a person is confident, but not arrogant. Respect for others is important to me. I appreciate an open mind. I want to fall in love again. I want to be someone's world, and them to be mine. I'm a romantic. Having a physical and emotional attraction to someone is critical. I love hugs, holding hands, spooning, giving (and receiving) back scratches ... intimacy.

That's enough for now. Still want to speak?

From: Tom Miller <happysmile4868@gmail.com>
Sent: Tuesday, January 3, 2017 5:11 PM
To: anniem@yahoo.com
Subject: Re: Hello Annie

Thanks for your wonderful, long, and sweet mail. Yes, I would like to talk more and see how it goes between us. I am very honest, and I am like an open book. You can ask whatever you want to know about me. Do you have Hangouts so we can chat here right now? Tell me what you think.

From: anniem@yahoo.com
Sent: Tuesday, January 3, 2017 7:23 PM
To: Tom Miller <happysmile4868@gmail.com>
Subject: Re: Hello Annie

Hey Tom, I don't even know what 'Hangouts' is – ha! I can speak this evening, any time after 8:00 pm. Happy to share my cell. Have a bit more flexibility tomorrow night. Which is better for you?

I quickly search Google Hangouts, which is an online instant messaging app.

I'll have to figure out how to download that.

From: Tom Miller <happysmile4868@gmail.com>
Sent: Tuesday, January 3, 2017 7:50 PM
To: anniem@yahoo.com
Subject: Re: Hello Annie

I would love to chat with you. So, we can talk back and forth. So go on Google and check out Hangouts. It's very easy. I believe you can figure it out. Let me know what you think. Looking forward to talking with you.

New friend,

Tom

From: anniem@yahoo.com
Sent: Tuesday January 3, 2017 8:13 PM
To: Tom Miller <happysmile4868@gmail.com>
Subject: Re: Hello Annie

OK, technology issue solved. I just tried to ring you, so it now works! Apologies for all the emails. I'm quite proud of myself that I got this to work.

Hangouts – we're now instant messaging

Tom

Hello

Are you there?

Annie

Yes!

I tried to 'ring' you, but it just rang ...

I don't even know how that works.

lol!

Hmmm, he suggested using Google Hangouts, so shouldn't he know how it works?

Lol

So tell me, what are you doing now?

Right now? Trying to video chat with you!

Haha

It says you are not on Hangouts ...

How was your day like?

My day was really good! Aside from the crappy weather moving into Philly, I got heaps done! Where were you today?

My day was great. I went to the office to check on some paper works (sic).

How long have you been single, without a man?

Where's your office?

Oops, we are writing over each other.

Brb. On phone

Brb … oh yeah, be right back. I had to think about that for a second …

Good. That gives me a chance to think about how to answer your question. Ha!

I'm here now

Welcome back! So, I've been single/divorced since 2012. I've dated two guys since then. Have been just hanging with friends the past few months.

What about you? You're a good-looking man; you must date a lot.

Thank you …

That's not an answer!

I have been single for a few years now and I think its about time to be happy again. Life is too short.

So, are you ready to be in a relationship right now? I asked because I don't want to be hurt anymore.

We should be speaking on the phone … I'm not a big fan of this Hangouts thing. Yes, I'm ready to be in a relationship if I meet the right person. Neither of us can worry about getting hurt at this stage.

Interesting that he is jumping right to a relationship question … is that how online dating works? I haven't even spoken to him on the phone yet, and he is talking about being hurt. He appears more confident in his photo than he sounds in his messages.

I want to speak on the phone also, but I would want us to talk on here and get to know each other better before we take it to the next level. I want to take a step at (a) time.

I believe time will tell.

No worries. Would just like to hear your voice. I don't consider a phone call a commitment ...

A phone call is 'taking it to the next level'? Holy cow! I definitely don't understand online dating protocols ...

I believe physical attraction and chemistry are important, but sometimes we need to have difference (sic) interests so we can learn from each other.

I am (sic) divorced for ten years with no children because my ex couldn't. Was married for five years and it was hell. My ex cheated and brought men to my house when I am (sic) gone for (sic) business trips and one of the men was my friend too.

Any children?

You do not remember my long email? lol

Yes, Jack, he's 26 ... a great young man.

Yikes, did he not even read my email? Or is he talking to multiple women at once and can't keep us straight? Definitely a 'note to file' for me.

I remember all that you said, but I would like to start all (over) again

I keep adding a year to Jack ... he's 25.

Since we are getting to know each other better.

I love children a lot ... I believe they are (a) blessing in our lives.

You are right. I'm sorry you did not have kids of your own. I had a daughter as well ... one year before Jack. Her name was Sydney. She was stillborn, a very tragic event. I still think of her every day.

Sorry for your loss.

I believe she is in a good place now. Actually, my dad died when I was 35 years old. After my dad died, my mum also fell very sick and soon she also went (sic) away. When it comes to brothers and sisters, I do not have any brother or sister. I am alone, but my grandmother and my uncle always call me from Portugal.

Were you born in Portugal? How did you end up in Pittsburgh?

I was born in Lisbon.

I was in New York before I moved to Pittsburgh because I wanted to be far away from my ex.

Do you like Pittsburgh? It's quite different from NY ...

Gosh, Pittsburgh ... why would someone move there? I know there's been a lot of investment in the city, but Portugal to NY to Pittsburgh ... weird.

I like Pittsburgh and I think it's pretty cool here.

Are you a one-man woman or are you are getting to know someone else?

Well, I only signed onto this silly site last night, as you know. I learned how to change my profile to private, because I didn't like getting winks and chats and stuff like that. One other man reached out; he lives in Syria right now! LOL! He's in the Army. I figure I might speak to others until I actually get to know/meet someone and decide to spend time with them. Make sense? Are you expecting to only speak to me? We live kind of far apart to put all our eggs in one basket.

Heck, he lives 200 miles away! Does he really think I'm only going to speak to him?

I'm not skilled enough to date more than one person at a time. I believe it will be very confusing dating two people at a time, so I would like to take one day at a time. So I must say I am going to get to know you for now and see where it leads, and when there is the need to go back on Match I will, but for now I am only talking to you and only you.

I think distance isn't a factor either; if the hearts find each other, they will find a way to get together. I must say though it isn't as wonderful as living within an hour of each other, as the hugging and kissing can't occur. If we can talk online, on the phone, or in person, it should all be the same honest conversation. Everyone looking seems to have their own idea of how relationships are formed. I truly believe in mental attraction equally with physical attraction (sic). I am a true person (sic). I would not deceive people, so you can trust that what I write or say is the real thing. So, distance can work to an (sic) advantage of really getting to know someone for who they are, not just for the physical attraction which can fade.

That all makes sense to me, Tom. I welcome the chance to get to know each other via Hangouts, email, etc. I am an honest person as well. I won't lead you on or deceive you. But right now, we are not dating. We are just two people getting acquainted. If you start dating someone, or I start dating someone, we can let each other know. Fair enough?

Strange, his image is fading out as if he's off-line.

You get a lot of calls! Ha. Your picture fades when you appear off-line.

Dating ... I definitely don't consider chatting on Hangouts to be dating. I'm not shutting down my profile because we started to chat. I don't even know how to shut down my profile!

Oh, okay ... But I don't (know) why. I think I will check it later.

So, are you ready for that special man?

Absolutely! I deserve him!

I am single, happy, and looking for a woman to spend time with and explore life. I love to spend time with people, friends, or strangers. It is good and brings energy. I love to travel but always want to go back to the comfort of my home. Nice quiet nights watching a movie or talking and sharing thoughts. Can I be that lucky man?

Oh boy, wasn't ready for that question ... how do I dance around that?

And you deserve to be happy and loved as well!!! Regardless of where this leads, I want you to fall in love again and put those old memories of hurt and pain behind you.

By the way, I love watching movies at home!!!

Communication and trust are the cornerstones of a good relationship. It is important to be able to talk and express thoughts, feelings, and ideas.

I love watching movies at home too. I don't have much confidence in the psychic abilities of others to know what I am thinking, so I usually say what is on my mind.

That works for me! I'm pretty open myself. Or at least I will ask a question if I don't understand something that has been said. This is also important when we're emailing or typing ... it's hard to know the tone sometimes.

One last question ... and then I must go work out. How many languages do you speak? And what are they?

I believe it all depends on us and how we communicate with each other. I speak English and Portuguese. You?

English, a bit of Spanish. A little French ... and I'm teaching myself German.

Awesome! I now have a teacher. Lol

Would you like to be my teacher to teach me how to French? (sic)

LOL! Do you mean speak French?

Sorry, I mean speak

Oui!

Haha

Do you know what you want in a new partner?

Companionship, intellectual stimulation, adventure, friendship, tenderness, passion, respect, honesty, financial stability, kindness. Those things would be a high priority.

What about you?

I want someone who I can talk to about anything, someone who would be happy to just go out for a coffee and have a laugh without drink, drugs, or arguments. Someone I can spend a lovely, peaceful time with without it costing the earth. Kindness, gentleness, understanding, fidelity, truthfulness, togetherness, independence. If two people lean on each other they will fall apart. They both need to be able to stand alone, only then can they stand together.

I want someone that isn't afraid to show affection whether it be in public or private. Someone that I can talk with about anything and someone that can make me laugh for starters. I want someone warm, caring, and trusting.

I think he has answered that question before...

I think we both want similar things ... except I don't drink coffee or tea ... so, we'll have to go to a place that serves Diet Pepsi or Diet Coke. Ha.

Oh I see

That's a deal breaker, isn't it? lol!

No problem with that. No, not at all.

Yes ... You sound very interesting.

I would like to know more about you.

Sounds good, my new friend, Tom. I'm glad you saw my profile and reached out. Oh, one thing. I'm 57 not 56. My profile is wrong, but everything else is correct.

And this is where you say I only look 47!!!

You are beautiful and you don't look like your age.

Perfect response! On that note, have a great night. Sleep well. I'll be working from home, so I'll be able to chat again, but not for an hour, unless it's the evening.

Okay. Let me know when you are up tomorrow

Ciao for now!

Goodnight

Goodnight, Tom.

He sounds like a nice man. Definitely has been hurt before, so he's pretty cautious. And he's also very straightforward about what he's looking for. Being on a dating site is quite an education for me. I'm not used to sharing so much via email or instant messaging with someone I haven't met in person. I would like to hear his voice.

Day 3, January 3

I'm Tom Miller

From: Tom Miller <happysmile4868@gmail.com>
Sent: Wednesday, January 4, 2017 7:03 AM
To: anniem@yahoo.com
Subject: Good morning

A great day starts with a good morning! How are you today? Begin today with a heaping (sic) spoonful of energy! Sprinkle it with lots of happiness, sunshine, and smiles!! Add a generous helping of optimism to keep you going!!! I hope you enjoyed your night. It was nice talking to you last night. It would be nice for us to get to know each other better and keep it going. I trust everything you told me, and I want you to know if you want to make a relationship work, you have to trust one another. And trust is very important to me. Let me know what time you will be online so we can talk and get to know each other more.

Have a great day!

Your new friend,

Tom

A bit corny. He definitely had major trust issues in past relationships. Gosh, he refers to trusting one another often.

From: anniem@yahoo.com
Sent: Wednesday, January 4, 2017 12:33 PM
To: Tom Miller <happysmile4868@gmail.com>
Subject: Good morning

Hey Tom,

I'll be offline at about 4:00 pm today. I had given my son tickets to tonight's Flyers game and now he is sick and can't use them. After making heaps of calls this afternoon, I finally found two women from work to use the tickets with me. So, I have to get ready for the game and then pick them both up in Philly and take them to the game. See, if you lived closer you could have gone with me! Ha!

Sorry we missed the chance to connect by Hangouts.

Tomorrow I have a client lunch in New Jersey and then a meeting in Philly, so I'll be on the road till the end of the day. But let's try to connect tomorrow evening. Will that work for you? I'm storing up lots of questions for you!!! Like ... is your name really Tom Miller? That doesn't sound very Portuguese!

Best, Annie

From: Tom Miller <happysmile4868@gmail.com>
Sent: Wednesday, January 4, 2017 3:40 PM
To: anniem@yahoo.com
Subject: Good morning

Please go and come. I would like us to talk more when you are back, and I would like us to watch more matches someday soon. Keep smiling. What time will you be back from the game? Let me know what time so we can talk. And asking about my name, it's Tom Miller. Take care and drive safe(ly).

I send Tom a photo of me in my hockey shirt.

From: Tom Miller <happysmile4868@gmail.com>
Sent: Wednesday, January 4, 2017 3:55 PM
To: anniem@yahoo.com
Subject: Good morning

Wow, you look beautiful. I would like us to talk when you are back and keep smiling. I love it on your face.

From: Tom Miller <happysmile4868@gmail.com>
Sent: Wednesday, January 4, 2017 4:05 PM
To: anniem@yahoo.com
Subject: Good morning

Wow, lucky you. I wish I was around so I can drive you girls and please have your son get some meds. You better do that before you leave. Email me when you get there or send me your number again, so I can text you.

All the stars in the sky cannot compare to the beauty of your smile.

Day 4, January 5

Got His Number

Good morning

How are you doing and how was your night?

I was just about to text you. Maybe I should stop lol.

Hey there! I'm tired as I got home late. After the game, and we stayed till the bitter end, hoping our team would somehow turn it around, I had to take one colleague back into (the) center (of the) city and the other to the northern suburbs. So not home till after 1:00.

Oh I see. I am sorry you lost.

But if I was to be with you together, I will laugh at you in the bedroom ...

Why would you be laughing? Because of my sleepy face?

Because your team lost. lol

No way!!! Who do you cheer for in hockey?

Don't say the Pittsburgh Penguins!

lol

Why didn't you text me last night? I thought you might since I sent my cell.

I love the New York Islanders.

I like them because I was born in NYC.

Ugh ... I guess I'll cut you a break since you were born there.

So, maybe you wanted the Rangers to win as a 'sister' team?

But I support the Pittsburgh Pirates here.

We will be a good match at a Philly Pittsburgh competition!

So maybe we could go together, huh?

Would love to! Now, why didn't you text me last night?

He has ignored my question. I'm not letting him off the hook.

814 263 5299

I didn't because I thought you were having fun

Oh boy, you gave me your number ... does that mean we('ve) reached a next step? lol

Yeah, I think so. And do you think I can be the man you are looking for?

Perhaps. Hard to tell through hanging out, so to speak. Do you have one leg and no teeth?

I believe we can talk and get to know each other more before we meet.

You can't take a day to like someone. Hope you know that.

Talking would be a good next step!

Yeah.

Tom sends a selfie of himself at home.

Oh man, tough questions early in the morning ... is that you right now?

I'm not used to such 'deep' questions. Another photo ... very handsome. He is definitely keeping my attention.

Yeah, that is me.

Successful relationships have some adjustment periods, but being hurt shouldn't be part of being in love. Loving relationships have good qualities, such as support from your partner, a willingness to communicate, a desire to compromise, and open and honest communication.

I don't know that I would use the word successful. Instead, I would say 'meaningful'. And it relates to the things I said I am looking for. The relationship is meaningful if we 'connect' emotionally, spiritually, and physically. If we are best friends and can be there for one another to celebrate wins and hold each other when we are sad. It's meaningful if we can be comfortable next to each other, even in silence. It's meaningful ...

You sound interesting

... you interrupted me lol

I AM!!! And very modest!

I'm laughing right now ... in case you can't hear me.

We need to be best friends and I would always give my woman the space whenever she ask(s) for it.

We need to be best friends first. Because that makes a relationship last, and people don't hurt their best friend.

Yes, and trust one another because without trust no relationship can work out.

'My woman' ... that's an odd way to refer to his partner ... and his grammar is not perfect, as if he is not fluent in English. Interesting.

I agree. And I understand why trust is so important to you. But forgiveness is also just as important.

In any organization with more than one person in it, there will be more than one opinion.
All should work together to see that both of you can compromise on different subjects. If someone isn't willing to compromise, they are not willing to acknowledge your wants and desires.

Yes, I don't want to be hurt anymore and I believe whenever you say it's from your heart, because I also mean whatever I say. I am like an open book; you can ask whatever you want to know about me.

I have to ask this ... he continues to talk about being hurt.

Do you believe in forgiveness?

Yes, I believe in forgiveness.

Do you?

Tell me what you are most passionate about in life?

I think forgiveness is critical. Otherwise we carry with us too much pain, hate, ill will.

I have to answer your last question later, as I have to get in the car and drive to a meeting.

But before I go ... I wanted to say you look very handsome this morning. Blue suits look nice on you!

Oh, okay. So you are leaving already. You text me when you are back.

I'll be driving from New Jersey directly to Philly for a meeting. I'll text you when I'm done with my meetings. It was great to talk to you today!

Sorry to dash ... I just saw the time!

Okay.

Take care and drive safe.

Be careful and keep smiling.

Always!!!

Later that evening....

Good evening, Tom!

I'm going to work out. Will be back online in an hour.

I'm back ...

Day 5, January 6

Limited Communication

> Hello, I haven't heard from you today

> Hmm, did you get my text? I gave an update on my schedule and asked if you were free to talk or 'Hangout'. Let me know your schedule for this evening.

> It's crazy that we haven't been able to connect. I guess we are both busy people. I leave tomorrow for a vacation in Florida. I'll be able to connect if you tell me the best way to get in touch with you and when. Please confirm if you got my text messages. Annie

It's a bit frustrating he's not always getting my messages; it's like we are in different time zones.

Day 6, January 7

_____

We Speak

From: anniem@yahoo.com
Sent: Saturday, January 7, 2017 1:45 PM
To: Tom Miller <happysmile4868@gmail.com>
Subject: Trying to connect

Please confirm you got this message. Not sure why our messages aren't getting through. I would love to speak!!!!

From: Tom Miller <happysmile4868@gmail.com>
Sent: Saturday, January 7, 2017 2:15 PM
To: anniem@yahoo.com
Subject: Trying to connect

Yes, I am getting it. I just got in from a walk. How is your day going so far?

From: anniem@yahoo.com
Sent: Saturday, January 7, 2017 2:20 PM
To: Tom Miller <happysmile4868@gmail.com>
Subject: Trying to connect

Hi!!!! Well, it's not going as expected. Jack was supposed to come to Florida with me for a week and backed out when we got to the airport. I went ahead and am now in Sarasota. Just waiting for him to call to explain what's going on.

From: Tom Miller <happysmile4868@gmail.com>
Sent: Saturday, January 7, 2017 2:25 PM
To: anniem@yahoo.com
Subject: Trying to connect

Oh OK. I hope you hear from Jack very soon or you have by now. I miss talking with you.

From: anniem@yahoo.com
Sent: Saturday, January 7, 2017 2:30 PM
To: Tom Miller <happysmile4868@gmail.com>
Subject: Trying to connect

I miss speaking with you too. When do we progress to voice? My tablet is running some updates. I'll be online as soon as that's complete.

I'm so worried about my son. I cried on the plane ride to Florida. The person next to me must have felt uncomfortable. When I got to the resort, the person who checked me in asked where my son was. That made me break into tears again. I hate being at this beautiful resort alone.

From: Tom Miller <happysmile4868@gmail.com>
Sent: Saturday, January 7, 2017 2:33 PM
To: anniem@yahoo.com
Subject: Trying to connect

Alright. You can always call me. I always want us to talk because communication is the key. I really want us to move this to another level. I want to be the man for you and make you feel special again.

Hangouts

Hi, I've spoken to Jack and am off the phone. Happy to connect at any time now.

Okay, I am here.

How is he doing? And what did he say?

You and I are online! Finally!!!

It's pretty complicated. He is suffering from PTSD.

And what is bringing him that stress?

What's wrong with him, I mean?

He was in a relationship and the guy got crazy, threatening, etc.

Oh and why is he threatening him (so) bad(ly)?

I guess I am not asking too much because I miss having a good friend and relationship with someone.

I am like an open book, you can also ask me anything that comes out of your mind and heart. I won't hide my feelings.

Life is too short.

Thank you. I have just been crying a lot today until Jack and I were able to connect.

No need to cry, Annie. I am here for you.

Jack's friend was threatening because Jack wanted to end the relationship. His friend attempted suicide and threatened to hurt me, too. All of this really had an impact on Jack. Jack is such a kind, gentle, loving man.

So where are you at the moment?

Oh gosh and why hurt you? Are you married? How long have they been going out? And what are you doing about it please?

No, of course I am not married. His friend 'spoke' of hurting me as a way to get at Jack. But nothing happened. This man is out of his life, but now Jack is suffering from the effects of it all.

It probably sounds like a movie.

Yes, I was asking if they were married not you ... sorry.

No, they were just dating.

What are you doing tonight? A nice handsome man can't be free on a Saturday night?

I am at home all night long. I haven't had anyone taken (sic) me out for the past four years now.

Maybe I will be happy again soon. Because I have a good feelings (sic) about us.

Big smile.

It's nice to be smiling again. I'm so worried about my son. It's perfect timing to have Tom in my life right now; to have someone to talk to.

Here's a question for you: how should a woman be treated? Or how would you treat me if we were partners?

A woman should always be treated with respect.

If you respect each other, everything else will follow.

Good start.

How will you make me feel special?

I am looking for the feelings you can't explain they are just there (sic). When you look into each other's eyes, there's an unspoken love, a trust, a real lasting connection on the deepest level. A single soul dwelling in two bodies. I believe honesty, truth and trust are words to live by.

Good answer. But there's that reference to trust again. I need to find out more about this man.

Tell me about your friends.

Who do you do things with? Who do you hang out with?

To be honest with you, I don't have friends I hang out with, only some few business friends.

I was born alone and have been hurt so many times because I don't have anyone to talk to me or care for me.

I feel alone in my life and I feel there is a space, but my mum and dad wants (sic) to see me happy, even if they are not alive.

What are (you) proud of in your life?

I'm really proud of my son and the man he has grown up to be. I am proud of the success I have had in my career. I am proud of lives I have touched and continue to touch both personally and professionally.

You?

Awesome. You are so loving and a nice woman. So are you inside your hotel at the moment?

I am at one of the most beautiful places in Florida, I think. It would be paradise if it was just a little warmer. Google Sarasota Resort, Sarasota, FL.

I am proud of my upbringing and being raised with strong values, which have influenced my life positively. I am proud of my home, good work ethic, happiness, and generally having a beautiful life. I believe life does not last forever, so my greatest pride will be for my partner and the true love we share.

Okay, I will do that and what are you doing there? When will you be home?

says my last message was not delivered ...

I'll retype it.

That was a great answer! I think I am proud of my upbringing too; it made me who I am. I like your last part about your partner. I booked this place as a holiday for me and Jack. I didn't think we would get time like this together once he starts working full time. I'm here till Saturday.

Oh that is a nice resort you are enjoying there. So, are you at the Summer Breeze or Santiago Bay? Just want you to know I looked it up.

The Country Cottage. Right on the water.

Oh. Awesome. I wish I was around.

So you will be home next weekend (on) Saturday?

I wish you were here too! Yes, I fly home (on) Saturday. And then I have Monday off for Martin Luther King Day. Are you going to be in the Philly area?

Unless you want me to? And you never know. I don't want us to waste one another's time. I want to meet and expect things to work for us.

So let's keep talking and learn more about each other. Tell me about your job. What do you do?

I work in consulting for diamonds and gold.

I took the business over from my father.

That's really cool. Are your customers jewelry stores or individuals?

Actually, when Dad passed, I was the one who had to take over his contracts.

I have some individual customers and a lot of jewelry stores

Do you enjoy it? What do you like most about it?

Oh well I like everything about it, but it's always nice to travel with your woman by your side. I miss those feelings so much.

Do you smoke cigarettes or drink alcohol or do drugs?

All of the above!

Just kidding!

I do not smoke, I do not do drugs. I might have a glass of wine at dinner. I did buy a bottle of wine for while I'm here. Let's see if I even open it! Ha!

You?

I don't smoke, I drink once in a great while, and no I don't do drugs.

Do you have any STDs?

You kidding, huh?

Just covering all the bases!

I am very clean and not even looking for a one-night stand. A lot of women on the site has (sic) offered a lot and I hate it.

What do you do for fun?

Nice change of subject! lol!

I go on holiday. I love to travel, take time off, because I work so hard. I take my mom out to dinner and movies. I have dinner with girlfriends. I invite my neighbors over. I work out. I take my mom to concerts and to NYC. I read. I listen to Adele and other female artists.

You?

I love Adele

Really?

Yes, she has a beautiful voice.

I agree! I saw her in concert when she came to Philly. She was AMAZING!

I love life's little pleasures. Strolling in the park or along the ocean. Spending quiet moments together with someone you care for at home. I love to dance, ski, cuddle, dine out, eat in, share feelings and intimacies. I am an avid guitarist with a big passion for music and my affinity for music doesn't only stop at that. I can sing too, but it's not a talent.

Wow! You play the guitar! That is wonderful! And you sing! Have you recorded anything on your phone that you can send (to) me?

I'll be doing a lot of strolling on the beach here in Florida. I also like to bike ride (not racing, just leisure riding) and they have bikes here. I'm a big cuddler. I love to snuggle and love to hold hands.

No, I haven't. But I will try it.

Do you play the guitar?

No, but my brother does. I used to play the organ; played at home for my own and my parents' enjoyment. And played in church for a while. I stopped after I lost my daughter.

What kind of music do you play?

I EXPECT honesty from others, and as such, I am always honest with them. You should know I will NEVER lie to you. Since I need to know that what you say to me is the truth and I can trust you, always that's what I give to you. The truth. Without trust, no relationship will last. If I tell you something, you can believe it, and if I promise you something, you can trust it. A real lasting connection on the deepest level. A single soul dwelling in two bodies. I'm a great listener. Someone who thrives on being that shoulder that we all need at times. Someone for you to confide in and tell things that only a special friend can keep private. I am sorry about your daughter.

I enjoy listening to great music. I like country, Christian, R&B, classic and soft rock as music choices. What's your favorite color?

Here he goes again with the trust thing. What is with that?

I really love green, but I wear a lot of black! So, my favorite color is not reflected in my wardrobe, but it probably explains why I love flowers, trees, the outdoors. What is your favorite color?

Can I guess? I guess blue.

Oh my God.

You (sic) kidding me. Mine is blue.

I should have said it first. LOL

LOL! I KNEW it!!!

How did you know it?

Did I ever tell you?

Nope! Just check the email chain above! I can read minds! lol!

What's your favorite movie?

I like science fiction, dramas, thrillers in movies and TV. TV, I like *Lost, CSI, Bones*. I guess I like watching things that take me out of this world and help me use my imagination. How about you?

Interesting! I enjoyed *Lost* as well. I watched it after the series was over and binge-watched it. I like sappy, romantic movies like *Serendipity*, the original *A Love Affair*, *Sleepless in Seattle*.

Aw, maybe we could watch these together someday.

So, do you have a passport?

Absolutely! I lived overseas and still travel internationally.

Favorite place you ever visited?

Greece.

What is (sic) your goals or dreams in life?

I have never been there. The photos are beautiful!

I love Greece and it's a nice place to spend your holidays.

You ask very thoughtful questions. My goal is to save enough money to retire comfortably. My dreams are still a work in process. My dream is to find someone I can spend the rest of my life with. Someone who accepts me for who I am. Someone who adores me and loves me with all their heart. Someone who will love my family and want to spend time with them. Someone I can trust, of course. Someone who will be faithful. Someone who likes what I like. Someone who will want to continue to explore the world and learn new things. But I want a partner who will be there if anything happens to either of us. I'd like to reflect on this some more.

There is a simplicity and harmony component that I have to also include.

Wow. Can I be that lucky man, Annie? I would love to be that man for you and be there in good or bad times.

Maybe, if you ever let me hear your voice!!!

LOL, or meet you!

The references to him being my man warm my soul. It's a tough time in my life right now, and he is making me smile and feel special. I need that. Perhaps being in Florida alone the next week won't be so bad if I can talk to Tom.

Meeting me is not a problem and calling me is also not a problem. I believe love comes to those who wait.

Ha!

My dreams are pretty simple really. I want to be able to create works of art, support myself, be in loving relationships, and follow my journey of lifelong discovery. My goals are to be financially stable, to be healthy into older age, to help provide a good life for my future wife, to laugh and love each other.

Nicely said. Did you have that prepared??? lol!

Gosh, it feels like he has answered these questions before…

Tom sends another selfie of himself at home.

I will always BE that special friend, but I WANT that special friend too!

I have since become stronger and feel ready to start a life of love and romance. I am soft spoken. Most say I look younger than my age. I am honest, loyal, sincere, passionate, compassionate and sympathetic, and witty. I love to laugh. It is so good for the soul. Love to dance and go for long walks. I like going out to dinner or simply cooking at home, going to the movies or watching a good movie at home.

44

Tom rings Annie for the first time.

He's finally called! I can't believe we actually spoke. But I can't connect the voice on the phone with the photos. He just doesn't sound like how I expected him to. He has a much stronger accent than I thought he would. Hmmm. And I guess being on the water in Sarasota is making the connection difficult. I don't have very many bars. That is so frustrating!

We agree to move back to Hangouts.

> Hi! I'm back! Thank you again for ringing me. It was so nice to hear your voice!!! You sound very kind. I too like to laugh; I haven't danced in a while, but still enjoy it. I do love walks. I must admit I have not been much of a cook. I'm a good helper though!

> You know, this little hotel/cottage has a private hot tub!

Yes, I saw it when I was looking at their pictures.

It's really a nice place to hang out. Can I fly and join you?

> You should! Be spontaneous!

I am very independent as far as I can make the right decisions and I like to bring home income to help out with having a really great lifestyle. I like to laugh, eat great food, dress nice, take care of my body, and go somewhere nice and warm, as well as go to a very warm and cozy place to spend vacation time. I like sports cars and own a Porsche.

We are very similar, Mr. Tom. I'm a very independent woman, as you can tell from my job, my travels, and buying my own place. I can tell you like to dress nice(ly). Even your casual is nice. I like that as well. We are both fitness people, which means we'll be healthy (for) a long time! Remember, my mom is 95 ... so I expect to live a long life!

ha

What is your favorite healthy food and favorite snack?

You told me you like Mexican, Thai, etc., but what is your favorite meal?

I like avocado and egg on toast as a snack. What about you?

That's a pretty healthy snack. How about an unhealthy snack?

I don't do unhealthy stuff, lol

Never????

Last thing I read was medical related, due to the fact I want to be healthy all the time.

I don't like a lot of ice cream.

Good, then we won't have it and I will stay slim.

I like to try all kinds of food, so maybe we can cook together.

Do you like a lot of ice cream?

I LOVE ice cream, but seldom buy it because I would eat the whole container at once!

haha

I also like cheese curls, but

I don't buy them either.

I would love to see you do that. I won't stop you.

Cheese is nice.

But cheese curls are not cheese!

I guess it's made of cheese.

I'm looking for someone who likes quiet evenings at home with candlelight, wine, and music. Who would enjoy cooking together as well as travelling and shopping. Do you shop for your man?

It's hardly cheese, so you're being nice. I love to shop for men. I'm good at it as long as I have the size right.

Nobody is perfect and there is no perfect relationship. You always have to make it right.

You are very philosophical this evening!

Ha. I miss those moments when my woman picks something out for me and I wear it and ask if it fits well.

I noticed your Polo label; you have good taste.

Annie, have you eaten dinner already?

Thanks.

No, I've been talking to you! You must be hungry and ready to eat as well.

What's your turn ons and turn offs?

Just asking you, and how are you going to get dinner, please tell me?

Great question (the turn on and offs).

For dinner, I went to the local market when I arrived and got fruit, cheese (real cheese), salami, Diet Coke. I'm set!

Good

Turn offs: arrogance, burping, interrupting when someone is talking

Turn ons: broad shoulders, blue eyes, 6'1", Porsches

Since you didn't comment that my description was somehow very similar to you, what turns you on?

Turn ons: someone who listens, who is interested in what I have to say, who cares about my wants and needs. Someone who puts my happiness before the happiness of others. Turn offs: angry people, people who don't take responsibility, narcissists, shallow people.

Oh boy, his answer is much more thoughtful than mine. I actually sounded a bit shallow.

I am turned on by little surprises, like a note left on a pillow, a back rub after a long day, an arm put around my shoulder when walking.

Aww, I have a lot to offer, just look forward to a lot of surprises

You seem incredibly nice, thoughtful and full of love!

Want to check out flights to Tampa?

There are two bedrooms in case this is a total disaster. Ha

I can't believe I am offering this man to join me in Florida! I'm half joking, but what if he offers to take me up on it? Am I totally nuts? Or just lonely? Don't worry, he won't take you up on it.

You're making me laugh here.

I can be too serious about life, so I'm told. A deep thinker. I love it when I can belly laugh. Attitude is so important, and I try to stay positive and enjoy being with those who live their lives with gratitude. I love to write poetry, a true romantic at heart.

Will you write me a poem?

I am easy to get along with, but I will say how I feel about things. Annie, I can connect with you on all levels. A best friend that I can trust, respect and enjoy spending time with, and if that all works out, perhaps someone to love and build a meaningful relationship with.

Yes, I will (in response to writing a poem).

Thank you. I will cherish it.

Let's give us a try!

Look at me, stepping out and taking a risk. I must admit, I'm attracted to this man that I haven't even met in person. I really look forward to hearing from him, and learning about him. Joking together. It's nice.

lol.

What is your schedule tomorrow? When is a good time to connect?

We can connect anytime since we have the phone and messenger.

Just keep me updated like boyfriends and girlfriends do, OK?

Will do. I'm thinking of hopping into bed and reading a bit before sleeping. I was up at 4:30 and I'm tired. Also, because it was an emotional day. Will keep you posted on my activities tomorrow.

I just wrote this poem for you. If you don't like it tell me; be honest. I didn't plan a lot of it.

My love for Annie is so great
My heart melts for her 'til the dusk of day.
The night is long when she's away
And together again, upon dawn's day.
Her beauty is great
My mind wondering 'til her I see
Loving is all I do
While waiting for the moment for her to say I do.

Read more about Poetry Generator: Create Your Own Poem by www.poemofquotes.com

I just created it.

So you can also create one for me.

Now wait a minute … you say you write poetry but use 'Poetry Generator'? That's weird. I don't want to be critical, after all, he did write this for me.

Wow. Thank you! That is beautiful! Me create one for you? I'm not the poet! ha!

I love art and world affairs. I'm interested in human consciousness and spirituality. I dislike bigotry, hatefulness, and judgement.

I always start with the dislikes. I dislike selfishness, disrespect, self-centeredness.

I love adventure, reading historical fiction, connecting with people, being creative, soft music, the smell of a rose, sand between my toes (corny, I know; no pun intended).

Hmmm. Awesome

I'm pretty emotional. I cry when I'm sad. I'm not a yeller. I'll get quiet when I'm mad, but will say what I'm unhappy about.

You sound like the type of woman I want, and I hope we don't let each other down.

If we're just ourselves, I think this is a match made in heaven!

I believe so

Are you an attentive lover?

Are you smiling?

OK, now I'm just being a tease. My sassiness is coming out.

☺

lol!

I can't wait to meet you!

Yes, I am a good lover and kisser.

Nice

I get that amazing flutter in my heart. I haven't felt that in a long time. I want to know more about Tom. I want to meet him. Can my first online match actually be a great guy? That would be incredible.

Day 7, January 8

Guarded

Tom sends two more photos of himself with this email.

From: Tom Miller <happysmile4868@gmail.com>
Sent: Sunday, January 8, 2017 6:37 AM
To: anniem@yahoo.com
Subject: Good morning

Good morning, Anne. How are you doing? I just wake up and the first thing I think about is you and I was thinking about you as I was going to sleep too. I love the way you talk to me, and I will be happy to meet you in person. As I woke up, I thought I would sit and write you an email about myself as you are not online. I think that IM moves too fast, and I need time to compose my thoughts. If you asked me who I am and what I want, I am looking for a life partner. Someone to share the rest of my life with. I have lived alone for a long time, and I have learned from past experiences and really want someone who I am compatible with to share the ups and downs in life. I am more of a planner and spend my time researching before jumping into a decision. I think these opposites can actually complement each other. I am very pleased with the outcome and it was worth taking the time. I am also in the process of buying new living room furniture and again I like to ensure I am getting what I really want. So, I have looked everywhere more than once.

What I bring to a relationship is this quality which I like about myself and has served me well. I am attractive and stay current with the times. I love fashion and staying current. People I know say I always look great and I like that. I am also a loving, kind, considerate, caring, and supportive person. I only want the best for my partner and do what I can to help my partner.

I am looking for someone who can do the same for me. Find a safe place to land and recover when needed. I am financially secure and like to keep my home in good order. I know that conflict comes up in relationships, that's what helps love grow, and I would want a partner who is willing to work through these challenges and find solutions by compromising and finding something that would feel like a win/win situation. I am not a very social person and have spent a lot of time alone and I like my own company, but I want more now. That is what brought me to the internet sites. Could you be the one?? I would love that. I would love to travel and see the world. I tend to like to spend my time with my partner, although I sometimes need time alone. I am an introvert, which means I need time to process feelings and just recharge my energy.

I love how openly you express your emotional self. You seem very clear about what you want in that perfect partner. I love how I feel so special when you communicate with me. It's wonderful. I am still curious about how cautious you are. You seem almost guarded. I am trying to respect your boundaries, but I also want to understand them. What are your plans for internet dating? Are you more interested in an email/IM relationship or have you some plan for how this will play out or you want to meet someone in person? That will be sweet because I would love to meet someone too. I am a cautious person. Like I said last time we chatted, I felt vulnerable about how open I have been with you in such a short time, just days. Not my usual style. I hope you are not married or hiding something. That would be a disappointment. I am an honest person and everything I have revealed about myself is true and accurate. In my mind, there is no point in falsely presenting myself as in the end the truth will come out.

Enough for now. Email me back if you have time and feel free to ask me anything you want to know about me before we can meet face to face. Hope you are well this morning. Email me photos and tell me more about yourself as well.

Your friend,

Tom

What a lovely email! Wow, he thought of me when he woke; that is what I said in my profile. Is that a coincidence? He wants to meet in person ... hooray! That would be amazing! He is picking up on my being cautious. But why would he ask if I'm married? What did I say that would make him think that? Gosh, I've been the one saying I want to speak on the phone and meet. Strange.

From: anniem@yahoo.com
Sent: Sunday, January 8, 2017 4:55 PM
To: Tom Miller <happysmile4868@gmail.com>
Subject: Good morning

Hi handsome,

Just re-reading your email. Thanks for sharing so much about yourself.

I am a peacekeeper, not a fighter. When growing up, I was the one who tried to settle my dad down when he got angry, even as the youngest child. I like to create harmony. I'm the optimist and the person who looks on the bright side.

I'm fun loving. I'm usually happy and like to laugh. I'm confident, but not arrogant. I have a thick skin. I tend to trust others first. I like quiet places: smaller restaurants, small gatherings; I like being with people I know, but for work I am fine having to meet new people.

My mom means the world to me. I want to be there for her. I want to continue to give her things to look forward to. I take her to church each Sunday. We're Catholic.

I like to work out and get frustrated to see how time is impacting my body regardless of how hard I work out. You should have met me ten or twenty years ago!! Ha!

It's important to me that you accept Jack for who he is.

I have two sisters and a brother. Maggie is the oldest, six years older than me. Then Paul, four years older. Then Mary, 15 months older. Maggie lives in upstate NY and is married to a man who is good to her. She is now a grandmother four times and has three wonderful children. My brother Paul lives in Texas. He remarried after his first wife died of cancer. He has two sons, who are married. Mary lives the closest to me and Mom. She has two sons and a daughter. Her daughter just got married this past June. Her husband is a doctor and works hard. She is a teacher. They have a special needs son who is very special to me.

So, that's probably enough for now. Hope you had a great day! I enjoyed my long walks on the beach. Wish you were here!

Annie

Day 8, January 9

The Crown

Tom sends a photo of himself with Miss America pageant contestants with crowns made of diamonds he sourced.

Wow, what an amazing photo! There he is with two Miss America contestants. That's a pretty cool job to source the diamonds for their crown. I never thought those diamonds were real. I guess he is financially secure. Note to file!

Day 9, January 10

_____

Getting Closer

From: Tom Miller <happysmile4868@gmail.com>
Sent: Tuesday, January 10, 2017 7:10 AM
To: anniem@yahoo.com
Subject: Good morning

Good morning, how are you doing and how was your night? I wasn't able to pick up your call. But I hope you know I was busy at that moment. So, you will forgive me? I just have some thoughts about you all night after I came home from a workshop. I want you to know that:

I will make all your dreams come true

morning and night, I will bring sweet love to you

All you want from me, daily, I will do.

I believe me loving and caring for you,

as long as the sky is blue.

Among a million you will ever stand as my only choice,

being with me will make you glad and ever rejoice.

You will ever be glad you made me your choice and never regret. And our days will be blissful with no divorce. Lonely, I made it through the night without you here, but I don't want to go through the day without you, so wake up soon and let's talk, lol. I feel much hurt whenever it happens that way. In and out of season, I promise to be there for you. If only you are ready to give me your heart, as I would like to take good care of your heart like an egg, so you have to know that.

In struggles of life, I will stay with you. Your strength and weakness shall be mine too. I mean everything I say in this mail, and I will be a helping hand in all you do. I wake up each morning and I smile. Why wouldn't I smile when I know my day will be great because I have you to talk with? So I hope your heart keeps growing for me.

God developed an awesome companion to assist me with when He created you. Destiny will forever have its way as much as fate does. We will be knitted together someday as the best couple in the whole world. I can't wait to meet you face to face and kiss you. I will end my mail here, so wake up and let's talk soon.

Your new friend,

Tom

Another beautiful email. I love the words, 'I will make all your dreams come true morning and night.' And I just smile as he says, 'So wake up soon.' How I do love to sleep in when I'm on holiday. And he will take care of my heart like an egg, so sweet. I can fall for this guy, my new friend Tom. Is this how online dating happens? The first guy is amazing, and that's it? Just like a commercial? I love waking to emails like this; we are definitely getting closer.

Hangouts

Good morning, Annie.

Are you there?

> Yes, but I had trouble answering Google Hangouts with video; I will ring you.

Oh, OK.

Do you mean, you will call me on (the) phone or what?

> I'm getting a message that I can only open the video chat on internet explorer, which is weird.

As much as I want to video chat, I just woke up, plan to bike ride, and haven't yet showered. I really don't want Tom to see me for the first time without makeup and my hair not done. When I realized how tired I looked on video chat, I just hung up. Yup, I'm a bit vain.

Oh, I see. You seem busy.

We will have to just chat; the video call is not working on my end.

Let's forget about it. I am here.

Phew, we can video chat another time. I'm so glad he didn't push to do it. I really want to see his face, but I'd rather look my best.

So, tell me about your workshop yesterday.

Well, it was a good one, but still not easy. I have the opportunity for a large project. I can purchase gold directly from a mine in China for a very good price. It would be enough gold to run my business for a long time. If (I) am able to bid a good price, I will still be in the race for the gold.

That sounds really cool.

Do you have other people that work for you?

No, no, I work alone.

So what does a typical project look like? Do you do design work or only provide the gold and stones?

Hmmm, another delay in the connection. Why does that always happen?

Shall we catch up later?

Hello, I am here.

I lost connection, but I think it's back now.

Well, I just provide the gold and the stones; that is because I don't want to design.

I don't want to add it to my work, but if it's for you I will do it for you.

I was just curious. I didn't quite understand your work.

Do you keep two phones? One personal and one for work?

No, I don't. Why do you ask?

Do you?

I'm thinking about getting a second phone. But for now, my company has a 'bring your device to work' policy. So my work phone is my only phone.

I believe the weather is about 21 this morning in Florida?

LOL! It's much warmer here. 54 degrees now, but will be 70 by noon!

Oh, I think he is referring to 21C; that's different. Why does he think of Celsius rather than Fahrenheit? He has lived in the U.S. quite awhile.

Oh, I wanted to get a new phone as well, because sometimes I have (a) problem with this old one. But I am kind of old fashion(ed) lol.

I missed talking to you last night, and I hope you have forgiven me.

How did you spend your evening? No reason to forgive.

I went to the car shop to pick up my car after an oil change, and got home late because I was expecting them to bring it to me.

I hope you get it back today.

I got home very late, so I decided not to call you. Because I woke you up yesterday morning and I felt very bad.

That's so thoughtful! I get up early when I'm working, but I love to sleep in when I'm on holiday!

I wanted to call you this morning, but I realized you might be sleeping.

Yes, it's always good for our health.

I had a great bike ride. The road I'm on has a bike lane. It's probably 2 miles one way.

How was your workout?

I have gym equipment at home, so I always try to work out hard and get into the shower. Have you heard from Jack?

Oh, got it. That's what I do as well. I heard from Jack on Sunday, not yesterday. But that is OK. He'll reach out when he is ready. I need to give him space.

Understand ...

Do you think I am asking too much about Jack?

Not at all! You can ask me anything as well!

Do you have some exercise machine (sic) at home?

Instead of asking about Jack, he is now back to talking about exercise equipment. Maybe the conversation flow seems odd because of the timing of when our messages come through to each other. It's a bit frustrating.

Yup, I have an elliptical ... can't remember the name, but it's a pretty professional one. I have a Life Cycle that I only use in winter because I like a real bike. I have a few weights and many DVDs ...

What do you use?

I use the leg machine sometimes.

I will try and draw a chain and an earring for you. So I will make it. Just for even if we are just friends or more then (sic) friends.

Wow ... that sounds amazing. I never had anyone personally design something for me.

OK, so I love jewelry. Is he really going to design something for me? That would be amazing!!! But he did say before he doesn't like design work.

I can do it for you. If you have any design you want.

So have you learned something about yourself from every past relationship?

Absolutely. Every time.

Let me tell you a few things I learned.

I begin typing quite a bit, so there is a delay until he hears from me.

Okay, I am here

Communication is critical, as you have said. When traveling or working away from home, connecting regularly is so wonderful. Staying close emotionally, even if separated by distance. Even if we can't speak, just getting a little text during the day to let the other person know you are thinking of them.

I have been in relationships when my partner did not stay connected; I didn't like that.

Yes, I agree with that because it will make the other person feel you are thinking about them.

Exactly!

Yes, that means they just cared about something else.

You know, don't get me wrong, but American men don't know how to respect and treat women right. Some of them.

I'm not sure it's related to a person's nationality ... I think it's related to their heart.

Interesting that he doesn't seem to consider himself American.

Because we are always going through divorce in this country.

If you know you don't love the person, why did you lie to them?

You are speaking in general now? Relating to the amount of divorce in the world?

Sometimes, I blame our self (sic), because we don't take time to make the right choice.

Oh yes, I am speaking in general. It's only our parents who were able to stay together and only death that keep that apart (sic).

I learned to be patient, so I know what I want in a relationship. I know not to take anything for granted. I also learned that I am a very strong person, very independent. I know how to comprise (sic) and play nice with others.

Those are good traits to be both strong and independent while also being willing to compromise.

Have you talked about your feelings with someone else?

Ever in my life?

Anyone around you.

I don't understand your question. Ask it again.

Have you talked about your feelings with someone else?

My feelings about what? Relationships? Things I have learned?

Yes, ever since you became single.

Have you talk(ed) to someone about the kind of man you really want this time around and how you are going to treat him?

OK, now it's clear. No, I have not.

Well, maybe I have talked to girlfriends, but not to another man.

Oh, I see. And do you think I will be safe walking with you in your hood?

Why wouldn't you be???

Because some men wanted you and never got you.

Oh, now that is funny! He actually thinks there are men in my neighborhood who 'want' me? Ha! No one in my neighborhood even speaks to me, except my next-door neighbors!

I don't think there is anyone in my neighborhood who wants me. So you're safe!

Would I be safe in your neighborhood?

Yes, you will always be safe, because I don't even watch the women in my neighborhood.

But I bet they are watching you! You are very handsome, sexy, and available!

I had a few ask me out, to be honest.

Believe it or not. I asked them to give me time and that was it.

Strange, right?

Just a reminder that I have a call at 11:00, so I'll have to drop off in about 10 minutes.

Oh, OK!

So, what time can we talk again?

So, tell me what sports do you play or like?

How about later in the day? I would love to enjoy this beautiful day. I'm OK at tennis; I like volleyball. I enjoy watching all sports, except cricket.

I tried golf years ago, but never had the time for it.

I like softball, if it's not too competitive.

You?

I love watching baseball, football, basketball, golf too. Nascar—I go and watch it at the California speedway when it comes to town.

Well, just text me when you are free and want to talk.

Perfect! Will do!!!

Have a great afternoon! Stay warm!

Stay warm as well and talk with me when you have a problem or need someone to talk with.

I'll take my phone with me to the beach so I can text you!

Okay.

Take care.

Later that day…

Here's (sic) some questions for you when you're online.

Tell me about your house. What's it like? What is the name of your company? Where did you go to school? From what did your dad die? What is your favorite cheese? Other than coffee or water, what is your favorite beverage? When we meet for the first time, what is the first thing you want to do? Lots of questions for you; take them one by one. Ha!

I was going to ask the next few questions last evening, but I knew you were tired. So, I'll send them now and you can also consider your answers while I'm still sleeping in the morning! So, what makes you a good person? What makes you angry? If you could retire anywhere, where would it be? What would be our first vacation together? Where would we go? That's probably enough for now. I'll be waiting for your answers, my new friend, Tom.

Day 10, January 11

Jewelry

From: Tom Miller <happysmile4868@gmail.com>
Sent: Wednesday, January 11, 2017 9:19 AM
To: anniem@yahoo.com
Subject: Are you awake yet?

Good morning, beautiful. How are you, and how was your night? I believe you are sleeping and smiling because you think of me. It was nice to hear your voice before going to sleep and I care and want to be the best man for you, but I want you to know even when distance separates us, even for a few days, what I feel for you is beckoned to the top of my heart. It's then I am reminded my already deep affection for you is continually growing. Missing you is a bitter, made sweet. There is no enchantment grander than what is happening between us. Like the poems, books, movies, and songs all say, I am no longer fully myself without you. We are falling in love. Nothing ever felt this good before.

So, I want to take time and answer what you asked me. Oh well, the square footage of my house is 2,688 sqft. I have 1 studio, 1 office, 2 baths, and 3 bedrooms so you will get somewhere to rest if you visit and don't want to sleep in my room lol ☺. Oh well, my company is Tom's Jewelry, but I haven't put up a webpage out there for some few reasons (sic), but I will explain when we talk. So remind me when we talk, ok?

You also asked about my school. I thought I told you how I was brought up. I went to school at (the) University da Beira Interior in Portugal. I study (sic) Business and General Art or what school are you talking about? If it's college you better ask me again. My father died from a heart attack. I miss him so much, but such is life.

I have gone over all of them now, so I am answering you one step at a time. And about my favorite cheese it's American cheese and Swiss cheese. Other than coffee or water, my favorite beverages are Pennsylvania Dutch Birch Beer and Dr. Pepper. I have a few more too!

You also asked what I will do if we meet (sic) for the first time. Well, I don't have a lot on my mind yet, but I keep planning for us. But first I will put my talking hat on, and ask a few questions and make our conversation grow, because I won't come and play it low for you to like me. But I will prove the real me, so we will have a wonderful moment together. I believe I do make sense. Well, I am even laughing when I woke up again and saw another question for me to answer, so I will keep on with it.

Well, what makes a good person? It's not an easy answer, but people who knows (sic) me very well, will tell you how good I am to them. To be a good person is to be honest, happy, respectful of others, and be easygoing and fun, be confident, be emotionally open to your loved ones, and take pride in yourself, and I think I am all of those things. I have already mention(ed) to you that I am honest. I will give you an example of being honest. Honesty is a way of life. It means you don't steal, you don't cheat on your taxes, and you are faithful to your spouse.

Here's a quick test to determine your level of honesty: You give a cashier $10 for a magazine, candy and soft drink. The tab comes to $8.15. Instead of giving you $1.85 in change, she gives you $10.85. That is, instead of a $1 bill, you get a $10 bill. You notice it immediately. What do you do? You immediately give it back; I hope I make sense as well. And also about what makes me angry? It's being ignored, fake people, liars, and I hate it when people criticize me and have no idea what I did. So, those are the things that make me angry and besides that, I don't get angry. In uncomfortable situations, I just walk away.

Also about where I will retire: Florida would be almost first on my list, but I don't know, believe it or not. I am not saying it because you're there, but I have been there a couple of times to play golf! And our first vacation together will be in Australia and New Zealand. I know you would love it. Babe, I will end this mail here, so we can talk when you wake up. I will ask you some questions as well. So be ready. Wake up and talk to me soon.

Your new friend,

Tom

Wow, what another amazing email. My heart skips a beat when he says this is what falling in love is like. Are we actually falling in love? I certainly get so excited to hear from Tom. And he makes me laugh so much; he seems like a fun-loving person. And he didn't mind answering my questions! Each one! Dang, he doesn't have a website. Yes, I admit, I tried to check up on him. There I am, being cautious again.

I then send a Hangouts message to Tom.

> Good morning, I will be here if you want to talk.

> I am laughing out loud! It's nice to laugh first thing in the morning!

> Thank you for all your answers! Well done! I also think this is a falling in love process happening.

Tom rings me, and when I answer, I hear guitar music. Tom is playing a song to me over the phone.

Tom: Good morning! How did you sleep?

Annie: Very well. That was amazing? Was that you playing or a recording?

Tom: It was me! Did you like it?

Annie: Very much. You play beautifully.

Tom: I'm glad you like it. Are you planning on going for a bike ride this morning?

Annie: Absolutely! I love to ride earlier in the morning before it gets too warm.

Tom: Do you know if they sell iTunes cards where you are?

Annie: Why do you ask?

Tom: I'm in the middle of working on something and I don't have time to go out. Would you buy a card for me? Is that too much trouble?

I pause and reflect on the request. I am still a little sleepy and surprised.

Annie: Well, I can look while I'm riding. There are a few small stores around; who knows? If I can find one on my bike ride, I'll get it for you.

Tom: Oh, thanks so much. No one has bought me something like that before.

Annie: No promises; let's see what I find without having to drive somewhere.

Tom: OK, call me or IM me when you get back.

While I'm bike riding, I'm wondering why Tom needs an iTunes card. What a strange request. And why does he need this for work? He never mentioned what value he needed, either. As I ride, I stop a few different convenience stores. I feel *like I'm on a mission. I need to find this card for Tom, for some reason. Finally, I'm told by one store owner that a 7Eleven down the road carries iTunes cards, so I ride there. Not knowing what value card he needs, I buy one for $20.*

Later that day...

Hey I am online. Are you there?

I found an iTunes card! Yippee! It's for $20. They had them at a 7Eleven. Here's the number you need on the back ...

So, what are you doing with the iTunes card?

Yes, I am here.

Thank you so much!

Are you downloading music?

Oh, I used it to download a couple of songs by Adele and others. And I had an app about my business, so I bought it as well. Thank you for buying that for me. I am so busy (sic) for work, it's hard to step out to get it. You saved me so much time.

Adele is my favorite! She has an exceptional voice!

Did you like my answers in my email from this morning?

I LOVED your answers! Very thorough, thoughtful, heartfelt, and funny.

You worked hard!

Oh yes, I did.

How was your night?

Very relaxing. I went back into the hot tub, practiced my language lessons, watched Obama's speech, read, watched a movie, and went to sleep thinking about you!

Aww, you are so sweet.

So, what are your plans for the rest of the day?

I'm going to go for a walk on the beach, come back and do some sit-ups, and then go to the beach. A tough day for me! What about you?

I want you to answer me, where did you go to school? From what did your dad die? What is your favorite cheese? Other than coffee or water, what is your favorite beverage? When we meet for the first time, what is the first thing you want to do?

LOL!!! OK, here we go!

I have a meeting at noon, but I don't know yet if I have to attend.

Did you already workout? What time did you wake up?

I work out two times a week.

I woke up around 5 am.

Yikes! What have you been doing the past three hours, besides answering all my questions?

I prayed and I do some paperwork; besides that, I don't know. And you have been on my mind, so I believe it's a good feeling.

He said he prayed. He must be a Christian.

That's really nice.

Did you want me to answer my questions for real?

Yes...

OK, one at a time. I went to Penn State (of course, remember the Rose Bowl night). I've got two degrees: Foreign Service and International Politics and Spanish Linguistics. I thought I was going to either work for the government or an international company. I had an offer from the CIA, but turned it down. My son jokes with me and says I do work for the CIA and consulting is my cover! Ha!

Any comments before I go on?

OK, I will continue to the next one.

My dad lived a long life. I am fortunate for that. He died when he was 91. He had a bad heart valve, so died from that. He had the option of an operation, but at his age chose not to have it because of the risk of stroke. I was by his side, holding his hand when he took his last breath. A tear fell from his eye at that moment. Very emotional ...

My favorite cheeses are aged parmesan and Manchego. For beverage ... I guess the question should be, 'Other than Diet Coke/ Diet Pepsi and water, what is my favorite?'

I love fresh made juice. I have a juicer and will make my own juice from oranges, apples, pineapple, etc. I am not a fan of Birch beer or Dr Pepper, but I will make sure it is in my fridge when you are here!

Sorry I keep losing connection

Yes, I can tell when you lose the connection as your photo fades; no worries.

Now for the most interesting of the questions: what will I do when we first meet? My answer is a little different from yours. I will touch your face. I will look into your eyes. I will listen to your voice, hearing it for the first time in person. I will kiss you. I will wrap my arms around you and give you a warm hug.

Now you have a lot of reading to do. All questions are answered!

Bad connection

Sorry alright

I can't wait for your warm hug.

I can't wait to touch your face and hold your hand.

I keep re-reading your email as I wait for you to be back online. No problem at all.

Welcome back!

Thanks.

I keep looking at your pictures on my phone and I hope you have no problem about (sic) that.

I can't believe I am talking to you.

I do the same! When I get home, I am going to print your photos!

I believe you mean everything you say to me, because there is no going back whenever we meet. I have great feelings for you and I will show you that I have a lot to give.

You will even ask me to give you space because I have so much love to offer.

I can tell you are a wonderful person, sincere, kind, loving. I look forward to getting to know you. Let's see if I ask for space. I am starving for love!

So tell me, what makes you a good person? What makes you angry? If you could retire anywhere, where would it be? What would be our first vacation together? Where would we go?

Oh shoot, there are more questions. I was hoping you forgot about those!

I am also starving for you.

What makes me a good person? I think it was how I was raised. My parents are/were upstanding, good people. I was brought up in a religious household. I am honest, loving, ethical, and trustworthy. I treat others with respect. I give people the benefit of the doubt. I have a big heart.

What makes me angry? The guy at work who put me down in front of my team!!!! Unprofessional, disrespectful behavior. Mean or abusive behavior.

I am 98% a cheerful, optimistic, happy person.

Retirement: I want to retire near water. Ocean, canal, or lake. Not a river, because they flood. I love the calming effect of looking at water. I have thought of retiring on an island, but there isn't much to do there and it's expensive to live. My ex and I still own a home in the south of France. That was supposed to be our retirement place. We haven't sold it yet because there were too many financial decisions at the time of the divorce. But if I bought him out, that would be an option as well.

Yes, I love the words you 'give people the benefit of the doubt,' not because you are a fool, but you want to see the truth in them.

Oh well, would you like us to buy it out?

How much do you think it will cost?

It's nearly paid off. It was a 15-year mortgage, so it's mostly equity at this point. We'll see. It's worth quite a bit, unless the market is bad. My ex just got engaged, so maybe he is thinking of buying me out!

Ha, I would like us to buy it out, if he doesn't. I hope I am not asking too much.

So he is engaged with (sic) another woman now? And does Jack move along (sic) with him?

What do you mean by does Jack move along with him? Does Jack like the fiancée?

No, I mean does Jack move along (sic) with his father very well(?)

Ah ... get along! Yes, they have a good relationship. Jack and I have always gotten along. It is a mother/son thing. Of course, when Jack was living with me, I saw him all the time and we got to spend more time together.

Oh I see. That's what I was asking.

Do you think I am asking too much?

Not at all! Besides, I am the one who sent you 20 questions last night.

I still have one question left to answer.

Our first vacation.

☺

I like the idea of Australia and New Zealand. You know I lived in Australia for three and half years from 1997 to 2000. It's a beautiful country! I have always wanted to go back. And I only have been to New Zealand once, the South Island only. And it, too, was spectacular.

You (are) making me laugh. Thanks and God bless you. So where does your ex live now? Closer to you? What will he do when he sees you with someone else, if we are holding hands?

I'll answer your question above and then get back to the vacation one.

Yes, Australia is very spectacular

And I would like us to work towards that vacation plan, because it's a very good idea.

I actually don't know where he lives. I know it's in the Philadelphia area, but don't know the city or address. He moved in with his girlfriend a couple years ago. We text and email about Jack-related things or financial aspects of the house in the south of France. We speak on the phone if there is something important about Jack. Not sure what he will think to see me with someone else. I guess he'll be happy to see me happy.

Awesome, I like that answer, because I don't want to hurt anymore.

So, is the house in Aquitaine or what?

Or it's in Corsica?

It's in France, but close to the Spanish border. It's on the side of a mountain in the town of Perpignan ... you get there by flying to Barcelona and then driving about one and a half hours through the Pyrenees.

I was asking because I know France a bit.

It's actually pretty amazing: a view of Mount Canigou on one side and the Mediterranean on the other.

The closest town (thirty minutes away) is Perpignan.

Wow. And do you want him to buy you out? So we can get one elsewhere!

That's a great question! Let's think about that!

I am thinking it would be so nice not to give the house up; or how amazing it would be to buy another property in France. I have never met someone who actually wanted to live overseas.

Okay we will see.

Time will tell, huh?

We are renting it right now. The same couple has been there for a few years, which is good. Better to have someone in it than have it empty.

That's a good idea.

Can I asked (sic) how much you are renting it for? If you think I am asking too much, don't answer because I enjoy talking with you.

That is a strange question ... to ask me how much we are renting it for?

Not a problem! Because it's a long-term rental instead of seasonal, it's 1000 euros per month. It does not have a pool, so a seasonal rental is harder, but it's also too much wear and tear. It's more of a home than a rental property.

Oh it does not have a pool.

I understand very well.

I don't understand why some men would leave a hardworking woman like you and move on with someone else.

I believe cheating is in their blood ... in his DNA.

He was not a cheater. We both share responsibility for our separation and divorce.

So do you have any tattoos and body piercings?

Ha! That is a great question! I was going to wait till you saw me in person and discovered that yourself!

Ha!

No tats, but I do have a piercing ...

I see. I like piercings, but don't get me wrong. I just like it.

Have you ever felt deeply insecure in a relationship? Were you able to name your fear?

What, you don't want to know what is pierced?

I want to know. So answer all.

You have a lot to answer and you can ask me as well. Ha!

It's not my tongue

It's not my nose, but you know that as you have my photo

I'm not counting my ears; those are pierced too …

It's not my nipples; gosh, that would hurt!

I like the nose. Maybe you will do it for me?

Ha!

That is a great look for a professional woman working in consulting!

LOL

That is why you stop working and we are by ourselves.

You don't have to do it if you don't like it.

I see, it is my well-kept woman look!

Tom sends across the picture below.

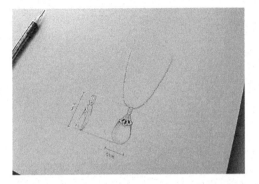

This (is) what I drew yesterday. What do you think?

You are an artist!

Actually, I'm not that fond of it, but I don't want to hurt his feelings.

Yes, remember I did art in school.

I have designed this necklace for you.

That is amazing. I would wear it every day with pride and love.

It's going to be a black stone like you can see it.

Yes, you can wear it anytime. If you want, I will surprise you with it. Do you like surprises?

I love surprises!

And I love jewelry, so you can never go wrong!

Yeah.

When was the first time you felt that you were in love with another person? What happened in that relationship, and how have you come to terms with it?

I will answer your other question first. Have I felt insecure in a relationship? Can I name my fear? Actually, no, I don't recall feeling insecure. I was afraid to file for divorce after 27 years; that was a big step.

The first time I felt I was in love? Give me a moment.

I guess in college was my first true love. We had a wonderful semester together. We spent a lot of time together. I thought of him all the time. We laughed a lot. As students, we didn't go many places, as we were in school. He was my first serious relationship! It was a long time ago.

What about you? Have you felt insecure? And when was the first time you were in love?

I do not expect a woman to be a servant to me, spending all her time working and cleaning; these are all responsibilities of a man too. I believe there is give and take in a relationship, but I'm not here for one's materials or other things since all these things are not included in a relationship.

Well, that is good! I work hard, but I am not a servant! Ha! And I am not after anything material either. I have done well for myself and have never been after another person's money or good fortune.

The first time I fell in love, she was very kind, smart, and sweet. We were too young (1st year university), and I did not want to settle down. Also, she agreed with everything; it drove me crazy.

Ha!

And I know we will move along very well.

And I promise to not always agree with you! Ha

Ha

Yes you always have to tell me your mind.

We are human and not perfect, so when I make a mistake, try to correct me.

Do you believe that past relationships should be left in the past and not talked about in your current relationship?

Actually, I do feel they should be kept in the past.

Agreed

Oh good!

Do you tend to judge current partners on past relationships?

No, as I wouldn't really have a good perspective on that. I wasn't there; I didn't know the situation. I will consider my current partner on how he treats me, my mother, my family, and friends.

So, when you are back from your holidays, how do you start work? Will you just go to the office from morning to evening, or what? And how many hours a week do you work?

Thank goodness Monday is a holiday and I don't have to start work till Tuesday. This coming week I have lunch meetings every day during which I am meeting my clients. I work 45 to 50 hours per week. With my new role, I won't have to work weekends that often.

I have a lot to offer you, the people around you, and I would never let you down

I believe that.

I have a lot to offer as well and won't let you down either.

Oh. Okay. I work 40-45 hours per week.

Thanks, you are so kind.

God bless your heart.

Well, not today! I just took up three of your hours!!!

Ha

I like it. If you were not here, I would be boring (sic) and sitting here doing nothing. Just wasting my hours with no reason.

But I have a reason to waste my hours.

I'm glad I could be of use!

So, I'd love to get outside a bit. And I know you have work to do. Is there a time later today we can continue to connect? This has been a fabulous morning!

Hey, I would like you to give me the website of where you are and the address of that place. Can you do that? Just email it to me.

We can talk when you are back from outside. I will be at the office waiting for you.

Yup, will do! I'll send you some pics from the beach. It will look the same as the other day, but I want to share it with you.

Ciao for now, handsome!

Okay.

Take care and let me know when you are back.

Three hours later…

Hi, are you online?

Yes, I'm here.

I have more questions for you.

When you get angry, which I realize is not often, do you yell?

I see you still have connection problems. While we wait, I'll ask more questions. Stay tuned for a longer note.

To be honest, I don't yell; maybe at my business client(s) because that is how it works, you have to be serious.

But I don't yell in my house.

Like I told you, I will just walk away and go into my room and listen to music.

Into your 'man cave,' as they call it. Good, I'm glad you don't yell. I'm not a yeller and don't react well to that.

Are you ticklish?

I don't know if I am or not.

You don't know??? How is that possible?

We will find out!

By the way, I had a smile on my face my whole time at the beach. I kept thinking of you and our conversation.

I am not a problematic person

Perhaps I spelled the word wrong. If someone tickles you, do you laugh?

Yes, yes, I do laugh.

Okay if I am a sensitive person, huh?

I can tell you are sensitive. I am as well.

Yes, I am very sensitive.

How did you know that?

I can tell by the things you have told me, the questions you ask, the look in your eyes.

Aww, thanks so much. So how has your day been today?

I hope that you are up front and honest with me.

You have to begin to trust me. My day has been great as I feel like I have been with you all day!

Thanks so much. I trust you and I hope you trust me too.

I will give anybody the benefit of the doubt; we are all human beings with the same red blood in our bodies, we all make mistakes in life, and I want to learn more about life in a relationship more and more. I'm just asking you to mean everything you have said to me and be honest with me, that way nobody is wasting his or her time or getting his or her feelings hurt. I hope I make sense.

Tom, I would never say things I don't mean. I am being honest with you. I'm a loving, kind, loyal woman and friend. As we get to know each other better, I hope the word 'hurt' is no longer part of your vocabulary, unless you fall off your bike!

Gosh, Tom must be pretty insecure. How many times has he spoken about trust and honesty? He must have really been hurt by another woman. I am actually getting a little tired of him bringing this up.

LOL

Thank you so much. I have a great feelings (sic) about us, and I will be a best friend and a lover. I can assure you (of) that.

The main thing is I just want to be totally myself with a woman, just being silly sometimes, serious others!!

I have a very soft heart and protect it at all costs.

I'm so excited about 'us.' I have dreamt about what you would be like as a lover. Now there is some honesty!

Wow.

You are so special.

Any news from the young guy?

Thank you. You are a very special man as well. No, nothing from Jack. But that is kind of typical. I expect I'll hear from him tomorrow.

Good.

Just asking. Don't get me wrong. That is how I am as a human. If I know someone, I always want to check on them.

I think that is wonderful. It shows your kindness, empathy, and compassion.

Any word on the possible new project? The one you met about on Sunday?

Well, it's still on going, but this (sic) people are very serious about the project, because there is a lot of money in there.

I give you a lot of credit for having your own business. It takes hard work, courage, focus. I thought of going out on my own (having my own consulting business), but I was too afraid. It was too risky for me.

Yes, I know what you mean, but I am doing this because I did not want my father's job to just end at once. I wanted to make him proud as a son. It's not an easy job at all.

I like to work with a group, so someone can watch my back for me if I am doing something wrong or if something bad is coming towards me.

You know the bidding for gold and diamonds can make the prices be very expensive.

Well, I have said a prayer that the business comes your way and I have my fingers crossed for you.

And I'm sure your father and mother are quite proud of you.

Thanks so much. God bless you.

So, what are you up to this afternoon?

I was waiting for a call from a client, but I am still waiting!!

Those pesky clients!

I don't think so.

OK, here's a question: which do you prefer, and you MUST choose, a head massage or a foot massage?

I prefer a foot massage.

What about you?

Definitely the foot massage!

When you are on vacation, do you like to relax, go on tours, play sports, or a combination?

Of course. We will go on tours and play sports, go for bike rides and so on.

We will have so much fun together!!!

Yes we will and I want us to share our love story on Match.

No way!!! LOL

LOL

It's so funny to think that we are both sitting at our computers laughing out loud.

Yes, it's feelings I can't believe. But I have always pray(ed) for this moment and I thank God it has finally arrived.

They say love comes to those who wait for it.

Yes, you have said that. But we both had to make the effort to sign onto Match. That was a big deal for me.

Yes, it was a big deal. It wasn't in my mind but someone told me to. I understand what you mean.

Well, you will need to thank them!

Yes, I will

OK, I have a very serious thing to discuss with you.

And I'm not joking.

And I know this is way too early to bring up.

Don't get nervous, it's nothing bad.

Okay, I am listening.

You can bring up everything, I feel like I have known you forever.

But, if we ever decided some day in the future to get married, I would not want to marry in the Catholic Church, or I would not be allowed to do that since I'm divorced, as are you. But it would require getting an annulment, which I refuse to do. Is that a deal breaker for you?

No, no.

Good.

Phew! No other tough questions for today!

I was born as a Catholic, but I know we have one God.

We will do whatever we want, (the) court is there!

Thank you. You seem very religious, so I had to ask. I'm Catholic, as you know. But I can't sign something that says my marriage never existed since I have an incredible son and a daughter from my marriage.

Yes, I know what you mean.

If I may ask, where is your daughter? We haven't talked about her.

What? He doesn't remember that she was stillborn? How could he forget that very personal and painful story I shared? I'm just going to be blunt about 'where she is' and see his reaction.

She is buried at a cemetery near me. There is an area called the angel section that is just for children. I go there on holidays and on her birthday.

God

Her name is Sydney. We just loved the simplicity of 'Syd.'

I have always needed a child.

I am very sorry, I shouldn't have asked at all ...

Why do you say that? She is part of my life. I prefer that people know about her and ask about her. I believe she is an angel today looking out for Jack. You can ask me anything.

Oh I wish I have (sic) a daughter.

What's really cool is that my mom always tells people she has 10 grandchildren, which means she counts Sydney. You would have been an amazing father. Your daughter would have adored you and she would have had you wrapped around her finger!

I had a stepdaughter, but I am no longer with her mother, so I don't hear of (sic) her often after her marriage. I will send you a picture.

Tom sends a photo of himself with his stepdaughter

> She's beautiful. That looks like a prom photo. Tell me more about her.

I was together with her mother, but things didn't work out because the mother was not feeling well. So the daughter had to go back to the father to be taken care of, so when she was going to get married she called me to come. And that day I felt special as a father.

> That's fabulous! I'm glad you have that closeness with her. She seems very sweet.

The sad news was that the mother passed away a few years ago.

She is (a) very sweet 23 years.

> I'm sorry to hear about the mother's death. Did you love her?

Yes I loved her, and remember she had a daughter, the same way you have Jack.

But it didn't work because of the sickness and I don't blame her. Life is too short.

I have always want(ed) to date a woman with a child. Because I wasn't able to have one.

But I could not stop her from going to stay with her father. I have no right to do that.

> That is very sad for you as her partner, and for the daughter losing her mother. I'm sorry.

Yeah I know

Remember, you could still have a child; you're a young man! Of course, I couldn't be the mother of your child. You'd have to give me up for a young chick!

Me with a young chick?

I haven't dream(ed) of that and how old will I be when my child grows up?

Pretty old!

Lol

I think you should keep me and Jack!

Yes, I will. I promise myself that.

Good! It's a deal!

Yeah a deal.

What is your retirement plan? What do you plan to do when you stop working?

I'm still formulating that. Since I'm going to live till I'm 100, I am going to have to stay active, busy, etc.

Maybe I'll be your accountant? LOL

LOL

I'm glad you think I am so funny!

I would like us to work together someday. Maybe a big jewelry company with our name.

Yes, you are very funny.

Hmmm our own company. What would we name it? Tomannie's Jewelry?

OMG

LOL

Babe, how did you come up with that name, just at once?

I don't know. It just came to me. I guess I'm beautiful and clever!

Yes, clever. It sounds good and prefect.

Tomannie's Jewelry is a nice name.

We can use it someday; I will pen it down.

I'm still crying from laughing so hard.

I like that you call me babe.

If we have a store, I will model all the jewelry; something new every day!

Yes, and if you (are) able to do that you will always be the face of our market because that is how it works.

I have been working with Walmart and all of those companies. And I know how it works. It's just a matter of time.

Wow, that's cool. That's amazing you have such big brands as your clients.

Yes, I have agents there.

Hope you understand when I say agents.

FBI?

Just kidding, of course. Are they buyers?

Ha

I don't have any problem with (the) FBI

LOL

Hey, do you mind if I step out again? Before the sun goes down, I want to walk on the beach. It's still cloudy, but 75 degrees. Do you have plans tonight?

Have you ever been fired?

Fired? Only from one client, not from an employer.

The client was a jerk. I was working on site Monday thru Friday. My dad passed away. I took off a few days; they had wanted me back the day after the funeral, so they fired me.

Oh

Okay, go and take a walk and let's talk later.

Will you be home? Is there a time that is best for you?

I will be home around 4:30-5 pm.

But you can call me anytime.

Perfect! After 5:00 it is! Talk to you soon, handsome. I'll be thinking about you while I walk. People will be wondering why I am smiling so much!

Take care of yourself.

Be back soon! I miss you already.

Day 11, January 12

The Ask

Good morning, sunshine ♥

Good morning, handsome!

How are you?

I just came back from the gym, but I miss you so much and you have been on my mind all night long. I want us to be a good couples (sic) and show the world all is not lost yet.

Did you get my voicemail from last night?

Oh, yes I got it. Thanks so much. I was a bit busy later in the evening yesterday.

I have been dreaming and thinking of us together.

> I wish this morning I will (sic) take you by the hand and lead you into the bedroom. With the lights turned off, I move close to you, letting my fingertips run up and down your arms, ever so slightly. Barely even touching you. I make sure I am far enough away that we are not touching at all. Just my fingertips running up and down your arm. I slowly lean in to kiss, but just brush my lips against yours and move to your cheek. You lift your arms toward me to embrace me, but I hold them down and give you a small smile. Wait, is all I whisper. I then lean in again and kiss your cheek very softly. I kiss lightly down your cheek to your neck. My hands are still gently massaging your arms slowly and lightly.

Tom's dream goes on for quite a while and gets more and more risqué. In fact, it is downright X-rated. I read along as he describes this erotic interlude, wondering how he is able to remember such detail from a dream. And as I read, I realize the English is perfect, not how Tom speaks or writes. It's very strange. About half way through the dream, Tom stops to send me a photo of himself, after working out, without a shirt. He asks me to send him a topless photo of me.

> You're handsome as hell, but I'm still not sharing a photo of me!

As I lay in bed reading his words about his dream, I also am shocked that in such a short time, he is sending this erotic message to me. I don't mean to be a prude, but where did all this come from? Is it truly his dream? And then, in an instant, the dream just ends, and we go back to our normal conversation.

> What are you doing?

What am I doing? You are driving me crazy! If this is even half of what it will be like to be with Tom Miller, I'm sold!

Yes, I have a lot to offer you, if you give me the chance. I would never let you down. God knows my heart.

Not sure how we moved from Tomannie's to this ... but that's ok. LOL

LOL

But in all seriousness, Tom, as fabulous as it is/was, and I will re-read it every day till I meet you; did you really write that? It doesn't sound like your voice.

I can't help but question if this is truly Tom's dream. It seems like something he took from the internet and cut and pasted into the Hangouts message. I'm just not buying it.

That is our dream company name and if we are serious, we can make it work.

Of course, I did. Like I told you. I had the dream and have to wake up and put it down.

I am not good at those things, but I try to make it happen in a good way. So I liked it when you said you won't share a picture of your body with me.

Well, that was the most amazing, sexy, hot dream! And thank you for respecting the picture part.

You are welcome!

What are your plans (for) this morning?

I think I better take advantage of this incredible day! It seems in this part of FL that the sky is only clear till noon and then the clouds come in. I'm going to ride the resort bike again and then head to the beach early to get some vitamin D.

What are your plans?

I have some meetings, but I really wanted you to do me a big favor, but I don't know if you will do it for me or not. Once I leave the house, I will be very busy, babe.

What's the favor?

Another favor? Oh, what will it be this time?

Are you sure you will help me?

Depends ...

I need to get some information on the project I am working on with this China client, so I need one app that I have to take care of it.

> ???

Are you upset?

Are you upset and not talking to me?

> Confused. Thinking ...

Thinking about what?

> Are you asking for another iTunes card?

Yes, I want you to get me (a) 500usd iTunes card for my project; I will give it back. I promise.

> I'm sorry. Tom. Please don't call or reach out to me. I'm sorry this didn't work out for us and you were not as honest as you claimed.

I can't believe it! $500!!! I can't believe he is just a scammer. I totally fell for him. Damn it.

Hey

Why?

It's because I asked you for the card.

Oh God.

I didn't know this is how you will react.

Gosh.

I needed this MATG SAP program; I am serious.

So you didn't believe me. Gosh.

I go for a walk on the beach. I have my phone with me, but I don't answer when Tom rings. He continues to send me text messages, asking why I'm so upset. I look up the SAP app on my phone and it doesn't even exist. He then sends me the following text:

This is my house address, if you have forget (sic) about me. We can still be friends. I am sorry for everything. God knows my heart.

301 Edison Street
Pittsburg PA 15106

I google the address in Pittsburgh. It comes up under the name of Rebecca. Now I'm really confused and upset. This time I answer the phone when Tom rings again.

We have a brief phone discussion while I am on the beach.

Annie: Hey, it's me
Tom: How are you?
Annie: Upset.
Tom: I'm sorry I upset you. I didn't realize I would do that.
Annie: I don't like it when you ask me for money.
Tom: As I said, I need this app for my project ... I can work without it, but it will enable my proposal to go through more quickly. Don't worry about it.
Annie: I looked up the app online ... I don't think you can use an SAP app on your computer.
Tom: Annie, just forget about it.
Annie: And who is Rebecca?
Tom: What do you mean?
Annie: I googled the address you gave me and it's under the name of Rebecca Miller.
Tom: You googled it? So you don't trust me.
Annie: You said you were divorced and moved to Pittsburgh. Now I see your address is under the name of a woman. Explain that.

Tom: Annie, let me explain. Rebecca is someone I dated and loved after I was divorced. She got very sick. It was cancer. She died. I didn't mention her to you, as it's a very sad part of my life. The house was in her name and she gave it to me. I am so sorry I upset you.

Annie: None of this makes sense. Listen, I'm not going to get you another iTunes card. I just don't feel comfortable. I only have another day here in Florida before flying home. Let's connect when I get home.

Tom: Sounds good. I will look forward to talking to you. Enjoy the rest of your days there.

Annie: Thanks, Tom.

Tom: Bye for now. I'll call you when you are home.

I spend the rest of my time in Florida cycling, sitting on the beach, connecting with my son, and reading. What an interesting turn of events. If Tom reaches out when I get home, I'll speak with him. But for now, I'm just going to enjoy my vacation. I re-read the messages from Tom each evening. He seems like a nice enough guy. And I guess I understand that he didn't want to speak about Rebecca ... it must have been too painful. We would have spoken about her at some point. I'm really not good at this internet dating thing.

A couple of days later:

When I get back home, Tom rings. He asks about the rest of my vacation. He apologizes again for asking for the iTunes card. We agree to start over and put the past behind us.

I'm so happy to hear his voice. I decide to give him another chance.

Day 14, January 15

Reconnecting

Text me when/if you are online. I'm just taking my Christmas decorations down. Wasn't motivated before Florida. Still am not motivated! Ha

Okay.

I am watching soccer now. I will text you when I am done.

I saw Manchester was playing today. Good luck! I'm heading out to meet a friend for dinner and will be back around 8:00 pm.

I am here when you are back

Several hours later...

I have been having problem(s) with connection and I don't know what is wrong.

So forgive me if I don't text or answer your calls.

Hey, handsome. I miss speaking with (sic) you! Sorry to hear about your connection. I hope we can speak or hang out tomorrow. I would love to make plans to meet in person.

I am here.

How is your day going so far?

Hey!

So great to hear your voice!

Hey, I am here.

LOL

Glad you have your connection back! How is your evening so far?

The connection on my phone is acting up very bad(ly). I don't know what is wrong.

I had a great day. I worked out, took Mom to church, ran an errand for her, nearly finished 'de-decorating' the house, and then had dinner with a college friend.

How was your day? What were you up to? Did your team win today? I didn't check the score.

Oh no it was a draw(n) match.

I have been to the office doing some paperwork for my work project.

Working on a Sunday, that's a drag. Do you expect to hear something this week on the new projects?

It has been a normal day for me, except for my connection.

Yes, I expect to hear something from them. And working on Sundays is something I have been doing all my life. I'm at the office so much it's like my home. I can easily walk there. I just do what needs to be done.

How is Jack?

Wow, that is great it is close enough to walk! Jack is doing well. It's my Mom's 96th birthday on Tuesday, so he'll be coming with the family for dinner at my sister's.

So if you drive two hours east ... where do you end up?

Harrisburg? Gettysburg?

Greensburg.

I am hours from Gettysburg.

Greensburg looks west of you on the map; just checking.

How is it that he doesn't know what is half-way between us?

Yes, I know I made a mistake.

What about State College?

Hmm, that is about 1 hour and 30 mins

And Chambersburg?

2 hours.

You know what?

What?

I can drive to anywhere you ask me. You are the woman, and the man has to make the move.

So you don't have to worry about anything. I believe you told your girlfriend about me?

I did.

So if the man has to make the move, how long do I have to wait?

You don't have to wait longer. I just have to plan and I mean re-schedule my time and plans.

I hope you understand me.

Yes, I understand. Well, get on with it! lol!

But your work is important and must come first.

Our work always is important and you know that. LOL

So what did your girlfriend say about me?

LOL Typical man; wanting to hear compliments!

LOL

Glad to hear you laughing!

I also told my mom a bit about you.

Yes, I always laugh when I am talking with you.

Oh really. My mother-in-law. ha

Ha.

Yes, I told her about the hot dream you had about me!

Ha.

You (sic) kidding me.

My mom is really cool.

Tell me you are lying.

LOL

I can't look at her when I see her.

LOL

And you told your friend as well.

Of course!

Oh my God.

Why did you do that?

I let them read it and I showed them your half naked photo!

You know, some things are for us only.

Oh my God.

Annie, you're kidding me.

Of course I am!!! LOL

Damn

LOL

Now I will be serious and tell you the truth.

I told them both that I went onto Match right after the New Year. The first person I met was this really neat guy named Tom Miller. I told them a bit about your background, your work, where you live, etc. And said I hoped to meet you soon.

I said I was speaking with you every day while in FL.

My mom liked that you are Catholic. Ha

BRB

OK, I'm back. So one other thing. My mom was pretty happy that I went on Match ... which is funny given her age. She knows of others who have done that and met people. So she was really supportive and happy that I am already talking with someone nice.

Not sure if you lost your connection or went to bed! ha! I'm going to head to bed now and read a bit. I'm off one more day ...

Tomorrow is Martin Luther King Day and my company is closed. So ... one last time to sleep in! I miss you!

Day 15, January 16

Widowed or Divorced?

Good morning, babe

> Good morning, handsome!

How are you?

I like how you laugh. You are very funny and you always make my day.

> Thanks so much and I am happy to hear what you said and I believe you.

> I am sorry that we misunderstood each other. I just re-read our exchange and thought you knew I was kidding. And I also said, 'Now I'll be serious and tell you the truth …' But again, I'm sorry for the misunderstanding.

> If I had shown my mom any of that, she would have had a heart attack!!! Ha

I had a crazy morning. My bank call me and said that someone has hacked into the account.

Oh no! That is terrible! What are they doing about it? Can they see who got into your account?

Not yet. They have opened an investigation. In the meantime, they have frozen my account. I hope they figure it out soon.

So you love living in West Chester.

I know a few places over there, and it's very nice around and beautiful houses.

I like being close to my mom. And I wanted to stay close to Jack's friends after the divorce, since he was going to live with me. It is pretty here, as you'll see. I'm closer to Chadds Ford, which is a bit less busy.

Have you been in this area?

Yes, I have been there a few times.

I like the area very well and I know Chadds Ford area.

What brought you to this area? Do you have a client?

I use(d) to have a friend in Radley Run Country Club. I don't know if you know that place.

Radley Run! One of my best friends' parents used to live there!

What a small world!

Yes, I use(d) to come around that place for golf.

Who knows, maybe you passed me on the street, or we ate at the same restaurant. Fate was beginning her magic.

Ha.

I believe a lot of things happen for a reason.

Radley Club is a nice place. I still remember there.

Maybe you will take me around when I come for a visit.

Of course! After we get to know each other better! Ha

So tell me, do you pay alimony or child support?

No, my ex was not interested in that. It was a pretty amicable divorce.

How did you make out in your divorce?

Oh I gave her what she wanted. We all know she cheated.

I called for the divorce and I wanted to be far from her, so I wasn't thinking about anything else.

Well, I don't have a child. So we did not talk about anything like that.

Can I still ask you anything?

Of course! Anything.

Did you meet Rebecca when you moved to Pittsburgh?

Yes, I met Rebecca when I moved to Pittsburgh.

She was very nice but wasn't feeling so good in health. I didn't talk about her because it was a sad way to lose someone who was a nice person.

That is what I expect from you. If you give me your heart, I will never let you down. I know how it feels. I am not here to hurt you.

I know when I hurt you. I will be hurt too as well.

What made you choose to use the description divorced on Match instead of widowed? That would have been a hard choice for me if I were in your shoes.

I wonder if he was intentionally misleading on Match.

Well I think after that, I went into a short relationship which didn't work, because I don't want a one-night stand.

I don't like the term divorced. I think at this point, everyone is just single.

Ha.

I am glad you hate divorce.

It's such a harsh word; sounds like a disease.

Can I asked (sic) you some personal question?

Ask away!

So should individuals within a marriage have separate bank accounts in addition to joint accounts? Do you feel that bills should be divided based on a percentage of each person's salary?

Holy smokes!

Hmm

When I was married, we only had a joint account. Now I'm undecided. I don't think that bills should be divided based on a person's salary. That is way too complicated!

I have worked hard to be financially secure as a woman. So this will always be an interesting discussion for me. What is your point of view?

Well, believe it or not, my father has always been doing that since my childhood.

I won't wait for my woman to pay the bills, as long as I have it. I will take care of it and later, if I need something, I will discuss it with my woman.

I think that is a better idea.

Well, if both people are working, I think the bills should be shared.

So now you have me thinking.

Yeah, it will be shared.

Also, I have seen in the past where if one person has, let's say, an addiction, then the bank accounts can be depleted quickly. So maybe I am in favor of a joint account for bills and separate otherwise. I have to think about that. Really good question.

What do you think of prenups?

Yes, I wanted to ask, because you always have to get to know your special someone's needs and wants. So when you meet, you will just move on with your life.

I think that is a good idea; you can have a separate account for paying bills only.

Interesting. He did not follow what I said about a joint account for bill paying. Is he not paying attention to our conversation?

And you can have a separate account for spoiling me!

LOL

I will always spoil you.

Just expect the spoiling part of me.

And I will treat you like you are the only person on this earth with me!

Hmm, you better mean that.

Because when you were in FL, you almost let me go away.

I know. That was a mistake ...

Did you know the main reason I asked you for the card?

You were probably testing me!!!

I did not have anyone to ask at that moment and I thought you cared about me. Trust me, ever since I lost my family, I haven't had anyone care about me.

I have always done things for myself whether (it) is good or bad.

So trust me, I need to feel that caring from a human being; I want to know if that real love that person has is still in their blood.

I hear you, but Rebecca and her daughter cared about you, so you shouldn't think there has been no one. And I know you have guy friends who care about you. I don't think you should feel so alone.

Well, I haven't heard from Rebecca's daughter in a while because the father didn't want her to be closer to me. I was spoiling her with goodies.

I didn't mean to take her away from him, but that was what he was thinking. And talking about friends, they have always been business friends.

I want you to be my best friend and lover. Can you be that?

Do you have significant debts? Do you gamble?

I do not have significant debts. I dislike and do not gamble. What about you?

Same here.

I don't gamble, I would rather give it to the needy.

And what is your debt situation? I would imagine a business like yours could be highly leveraged.

Have you ever used money as a way of controlling a relationship? Has anyone ever tried to control you with money?

My ex tried to control my spending, but I was uncontrollable! Ha!

About my debt situation. I don't live beyond my means. So I don't owe much.

I don't use money in a relationship.

I believe money is the roots of all evils. And it can let you lose something you don't expect.

But I am glad you didn't let him control you.

I had to submit all my receipts at the end of the week so he could complete the budget! That did not go over well. I ultimately refused!

Ha. Well, I believe it will be fun to be around you.

We think alike and sometimes disagree on some things and I like that.

I think we will laugh a lot, be very physical, enjoy just being together. We will challenge each other and have healthy debates from time to time. I so look forward to spending time together!

I look forward for (sic) the same thing, Annie.

So, did you play any sports growing up?

For me, no organized sports except in school. In the summer I swam, in winter skating, tobogganing.

Ice skating?

Yes.

Have you tried it?

I love ice skating and inline skating!

I used to skate every weekend when in high school. It was what a group of us did. I just got new inline skates that I'm dying to try; just need it to warm up.

I am not really fond of inline skating.

You had a lot of fun in your childhood days.

I'm still a child!

Ha.

So were you a good student?

Oh dear lord. Straight As.

Oh my!

My parents were both teachers, so nothing lower than an A was acceptable.

Wow that's wonderful. As for me, above average.

B plus?

Oh you are lucky because you always have to learn.

Yes B plus.

I was a pretty serious student even in college. Always went to those 8am classes when my roommate slept in. But had a lot of fun too; burned the candle at both ends, as they say.

Do you paint?

Yes, I do paint and do all the housework.

I mean, do you paint pictures?

Yes

Water color? Oil?

Oil.

Have you seen my room wallpaper?

Just went back and looked at your photo; the walls are painted a cream color.

Nope not that one.

Hold on.

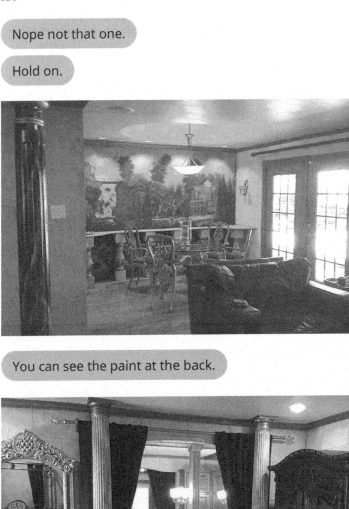

You can see the paint at the back.

They look like they are from a magazine!

You painted the mural and did the faux work on the walls?

Yes!

And painted the artwork on the ceilings?

It's never a magazine. That is my home. I had always wanted to share (it) with you.

Yes I painted everything. That is why I told you. I love art.

So where was the photo taken of you bare chested? That room is empty!

Ha. That is the room to the basement where I train.

You see the ceiling is the same, but no art on that one because it's almost outside the room.

Did you just design it or also paint it yourself? Either way, it is beautiful!

The paint was from Italy.

You have a beautiful home! You should be very proud.

Yes I am always proud, but not when I am all alone.

I know you also live in a beautiful home in West Chester.

Because I know West Chester so well.

Yes, it is beautiful as well, but decorated in a very different style from yours. I'll have to send photos from my phone. Shall I share as well?

Yes I would love it.

OK, hold on my bed isn't made because I am still in it! Ha! Maybe I'll make it real fast!

Alright I am all yours!

Do you read often? If so, what books have you enjoyed recently?

Just finished taking pictures. Decided not to make my bed, since that is where I'm sitting right now. Sending through to your phone now.

OK, check your phone. I told you my tree was still up!

So I just saw the tree you are talking about lol

I do enjoy reading. Just finished *Germany, Memoirs of a Nation* and *Girl on the Train*. Two very different books. One is history and one is (a) fiction/murder mystery. My favorite was *Pillars of the Earth*. And I'm a *NY Times* junkie. What about you?

Wow, you have a very clean house and I like it.

It's very beautiful and you have everything in order. So do you clean the house by yourself?

Yes, I do clean it myself. I had a cleaning lady when I was in my bigger house, but she never did it as well as me. So since I moved, I do it myself.

Yes, all the time. *A Thousand Splendid Suns*, a great story about difficult life in Afghanistan. *The Bell Jar* - groundbreaking for its time.

I will help you do it, when I am with you or you can call me on the weekend, if you want to clean. And I will come around and help.

I mean it.

If you are here, you won't be cleaning, I can assure you! Ha

I'm ready for a new book, do you recommend *The Bell Jar*?

Yes you can go for it.

It's a nice one. I believe you will love it.

I'll download it today and start it as soon as I finish the one I'm on. Then we can discuss it!

Alright I will be here, babe

Day 16, January 17

Killer Miller

Are you free to hang out?

Today is my mom's birthday.

Have to get candles for the cake, so must leave my house now. I'll ring you as I drive to my mom's.

I ring Tom when I pick up my mom to take her to my sister's for dinner. Tom wishes her a happy birthday. My mom has trouble understanding him. I begin to think again about his background and nationality. Am I so accepting because I lived and worked overseas? While at my sister's, I talk about meeting Tom and the conversations we have been having. My sister Mary is very skeptical. She says, "How can you believe he is who he says he is? How can you believe anything he tells you?" I just say to her that you have to have some level of trust when you meet someone online.

Later that evening...

Hi!

I'm on ...

Hello my new best friend, and

future lover.

Hello babe.

I am here.

Hooray!

Someone walked in to get something from me.
So I was attending to him.

Sorry for the wait.

No worries. Now, about my sister ...

Remember, I'm the youngest of the kids, so
my siblings are very protective.

My sister's name is Mary (I have another sister
Maggie and a brother Paul).

Whenever I meet someone new, Mary always
asks a million questions. She is MORE cautious
than me!

Oh you are blessed. I would love to meet them
someday soon.

Oh that is nice of her. She needs to be
protective and that is what they are there for.

To always watch each other's back, so I love
that idea.

You say that now, but wait till you hear the
questions she asked me!

You made my day when you gave me the chance to talk with your mother. I was so grateful. Thanks so much.

Okay I am waiting tell me. LOL

Of course, she is just plain nervous that I met someone online. She asked what you do for a living. Have I googled your company to make sure it exists. To be careful when meeting you. Make sure other people are around, etc., etc.

How can I be sure I can trust you?

How do I know what you say is the truth?

Wow, that's awful

I told you she was protective!

Relationships without trust can't exist. Because it's important to believe in things not seen.

So if you don't have faith in what you are doing, how can you get there?

In terms of what to do, you could promise her not to murder, beat, or rape me. Agree to a lie detector test. Submit your CV. LOL!

I AM JOKING OF COURSE!

Oh I swear on my life, I will never hurt you or any other woman in my life because I have never done that before.

I believe you!

A man like (sic) my type, I won't rape a woman.

You know, I don't want anything to happen between us again.

Because if it works out for us or it doesn't I will (sic) still love to meet you. But also I know it will work out, but sometimes women like to talk too much.

They can't hide their feelings.

Well, that is my sister! A million questions! Just very cautious and protective. She is risk averse.

She only wants the best for me.

Oh. Okay. And cautiousness kills a cat. In this life we have to take risk(s).

We are never so vulnerable than when we trust someone, but paradoxically, if we cannot trust, neither can we find love or joy.

Well said!

Now my brother; he will be easier.

A blessed thing it is for any man or woman to have a friend, one human soul whom we can trust utterly who knows the best and worst of us and who loves us in spite of all our faults.

Another truth.

So what faults do you have?

I don't know my fault(s) unless you tell me.

I make mistakes but I am a human.

Really? That's it?

So tell me, do you trust me?

I have no reason not to.

You know what hurt me the most?

I think so.

Oh, he is going to again bring up the fact that I Googled his address and questioned why he needed the iTunes card.

No one has ever cared for me before. Unless my family.

But I don't blame anyone. I don't choose well. But I think this time Gods (sic) hands are around our relationship.

It's so hard for me to believe that only your family cared for you. I believe what you say, but it does not sound possible, given what I know of you so far. You seem to have such a big heart.

Yes I have a big heart, because I have traveled around the world. And (I) know what other people go through. I know life is not easy. So you have to love and treat people the way you want to be treated.

The golden rule!

Yeah

So, when would you like to meet? I need to plan in advance only because of my mom, as I usually do things with her on weekends.

I really want to meet Tom in person. Talking on the phone and 'hanging out' is not enough. If I meet him, then I will know if he is an honest person.

Yes, I will know everything this week after the meeting is done.

If you had done what I told you to do for me, things would have been easy, but don't worry.

That's not very nice ...

Yikes! If I had done what he told me? You mean buy a $500 iTunes card? Here we go again! I can't believe he is putting this on me.

??

Just reacting to your sentence, 'If you had done what I told you to do ... '

Yes I would have known more about the process by now. But I am not blaming you.

Not sure you could have bought the app anyway. When I went online, it said the app was no longer available through the app store, but that is in the past now. I would like to forget it.

I looked up the app MATG SAP, and it was no longer available for purchase. Plus, it had nothing on the website that related to responding to proposals.

So do (you) have any sexually transmitted diseases?

I already answered that!!! Are you asking other women this question so you have forgotten my answer? LOL

Hmmm, is Tom talking to other women? Is that how internet dating works? And look at how quickly he changed the subject.

No I am not talking to anyone. I am a one woman man.

Maybe I don't remember your answer. I would not have asked again.

I am clean as a whistle, as they say!

Actually, I may not have answered that for myself before. I asked you and you answered.

I guess, because I can see it in your face. Healthy.

As a horse!

Ha.

Anytime you want to have a test, I am ready.

So now you understand I don't rape.

I am even scared of my life.

???

One funny story. A man went to a hotel with a lady and after they finished having sex, the man gave the woman some $$$$, but later, when the woman left, the man took the phone and called her, saying, 'The money I gave you was all fake.' And the lady also said, 'The pussy you fucked was HIV!'

Ha

I actually didn't think the joke was funny.

LOL

So you never know what you are walking into, so I would never rape an innocent woman.

May God forgive me, even if I think of that.

So remember, I'm a good Catholic girl. I have to go out with you at least 3 times before I'll let you kiss me.

Hmm.

I see.

Let's see if it will happen. You will let me kiss you as soon as you see me. LOL

So are you romantic?

I'm still laughing at the previous comments ...

LOL

Yes, I am helplessly romantic!!!

I'm also a very physical person.

Hmmm I am very romantic as well.

I will always want us to be touching.

I am ready for that.

I also love planning surprise getaways, and all I tell you is the temperature and how many days to pack for.

I am an independent man and I would like the same. Ballroom dancing is one of my greatest passions and I have recently started taking classes but I now need a partner to practice with. So if you don't have two left feet and would like to join me in my adventures?

I would love to!!! My sister Maggie and her husband ballroom dance and even compete!

You see, so we will have a lot of fun. If they find out we are doing it (sic).

You are incredible and seem to be the woman I have been missing for so long.

It is incredible how connected I already feel with you, without having seen you in person. You are incredible as well, Tom Miller. I am so lucky we have connected. I will always be grateful that you reached out.

A great relationship is the glue that holds everything else together. Comfort also means that you know you have and will continue to do zany, unpredictable things. Share the ups and downs in life no matter what. Not to be alone anymore.

Indeed. Gosh, can you imagine if we lived closer together? We would have kissed by now!

I can't wait to be in your arms. To laugh together, have you wipe (away) my tears. To share successes and things that don't go according to plan. Even with a family and many close friends, I feel lonely as well at times.

Yes we would have done more than kissing.

We would have driven Mom together.

LOL

Yes I know you will feel lonely when you go to your family without your right-hand man.

That makes you special as a woman.

And it's everyone's dream.

Yes, we definitely would have done more than kissing. Gosh, adult relationships are so nice! Sometimes it is hard to do family things without a man. But as you, I'm independent and used to it. Or I bring someone who is purely a friend, but that is not the same as bringing a life companion.

Yes I agree a companion is the word.

I have a dear friend coming over to visit tonight. I haven't seen her in several months. So I'll have to drop off of Hangouts soon. Until then, here's another question for you: are you circumcised?

So how long is your friend staying? And I hope you don't tell her much about me. Is she married?

Your answer, please ...

Yes I am circumcised.

Do you want to see it?

No, not now!

LOL. But I am circumcised, so don't worry at all.

So my girlfriend who is coming over is named Jane. I have known her for over 40 years! Yes, she is married. I am very close to her whole family. Her parents adopted me, so to speak.

She arrives around 7:00 pm, I think. And I think she is just staying tonight. She is doing some work in the area and wanted to spend the night here. I love her to death and can't wait to see her.

Aww, I am glad you will have some company today.

Honey, I have to get going now.

It's getting late. I will call you when I get home. If you want us to talk online, you let me know. I would love to hear your voice as well.

OK, sweetheart.

Bye for now, new best friend, Tom.

My visit with Jane

We had so much to catch up on, like her family and her mom, and the same for me, as well as my new love. I showed her all the photos I had of Tom Miller from Match and what he had sent to me. Since she is an artist, I shared the photos of the painting he had done, as well as how he decorated his house. I told her about my sister's concerns that I shouldn't trust Tom, as I hadn't even met him in person and I couldn't be sure he was who he said he was. Because of that, Jane nicknamed him Killer Miller.

Day 17, January 18

Address Request

I'm online.

Hello! Can you send me your work address?

1300 Chestnut Street, Philadelphia, PA 19104. Why do you want that?

You'll see. I have good news. I won the project for the work in Asia! I'm flying to Hong Kong this weekend! I have to work with my travel agent to make my arrangement(s) right away.

That is wonderful! I am so happy for you! How long will you be there?

It's hard to say at this point. I need to meet the people there and work through the contract. I'll keep you posted. How would you like to meet in Philadelphia? I can fly home via Philly and you can pick me up.

Oh my, that would be amazing! I would love to pick you up at the airport! How will you get back to Pittsburgh?

If you want, you can drive me back, that way you can see where I live. We can spend some time together and then you can drive home.

That would be amazing! We'll make it work!

I have many plans to make. I'll ring you once I have the travel figured out. I am so happy to share this news with you. Will you be in the office on Friday?

Yes, for sure. What do you have planned? I'm quite curious.

Oh nothing. I was just trying to know your schedule. I better get going. I have lots to do over the next couple (of) days. Sleep well.

Congrats again! Goodnight, new best friend.

Goodnight!

Oh my goodness! Tom won his big contract! I'm so happy for him! And he will come back from Hong Kong through Philly and I'll meet him! It will be so amazing to meet him at the airport! I am so excited! Finally, we will meet!

Day 19, January 20

I Love You

I had lunch in the city with a work friend. I told her about Tom Miller, how we had met, the conversations we had had the past couple weeks, and that he'd asked for my work address. She wondered if he was going to surprise me at the office; have us meet there for the first time before his trip to Hong Kong. I mentioned that he had already traveled to DC and would be going to Hong Kong that evening. We were both rather giddy at lunch, wondering what Tom had in mind.

When I took out my phone after lunch, I saw I had missed a number of calls; one from Tom. He had left a message asking if I was in the office. I told my friend we needed to dash back to the office to see what was going on. During the walk back, I hoped I would see Tom in the office lobby waiting for me. I imagined running to him, and falling into his arms, giving him an amazing hug and kiss.

When we arrived at the lobby, it was clear there was no Tom Miller there. My heart sank. But at the reception desk I was told to wait a moment as there was a delivery for me. My friend and I were so excited as we waited for the receptionist to return.

And then I saw the surprise. Tom had sent flowers to my office. A beautiful bouquet of white and pink roses. It was simple, but elegant. And there was a note card with a message that took my breath away: 'I need you in my life more than you can think of. So remember I care and love you. So it's my surprise.'

I took the bouquet to my office and called Tom straight away to thank him. He repeated how he had fallen in love with me, even without having met me. This was incredible. I was so happy. When does this ever happen?

I asked Tom where he was staying in DC. He was shocked by that question and said he was flying to Hong Kong that day. Tom had sent me his itinerary from www.checkmytrip.com and I explained he was not flying to Hong Kong till the next day. He had not noticed that!

I guess that can happen. You don't realize the time difference in the flights. It was a good thing I had noticed, as Tom would need a hotel in DC that night and it was the day of the women's march in DC, so it would be crowded.

Day 20, January 21

Gold Bars

Good morning, I am sorry for waking you up. I thought you were up.

Never apologize for that.

I wanted to speak with you. If it's the weekend, I sleep in a bit. I have some questions for you.

Aww, I am ready to answer it with honesty.

Some are more practical, like do you know the hotel where you are staying in Beijing?

To be honest, I don't know. I was in a hurry because it has been something I have been looking forward to a long time.

I should have come to DC after work and stayed with you last night.

Aww, it would have been great. I just learnt the air in Beijing is not so good!

Yeah, sometimes the smog is pretty heavy. People wear those white masks.

Maybe it will be clearer because it's winter.

Let's hope so, but I don't want anything to happen to me.

You have to give my number as the emergency number! I am your family now!

Aww, God bless you for saying that to me.

So, tell me about the project in China. What is the work?

Yes, but the business will take place in Hong Kong, that is what I know.

Even better.

But what did they hire you for?

They didn't hire me. There is a gold mine there.

Yes, so what is your role in this; did you buy the land?

Nope, I didn't buy the land, there is this big Chinese mining company that has the big share of the land. It is called Zinjin Mining.

OK, so I'll be Googling Zinjin Mining in a moment...

Oh, so you have access to the gold that is mined?

Yes I have access to the gold that is mined. And they will cut them into bars for me.

That is fascinating. How will you get the gold home? And how do you know you can trust these people?

Honey, trust me, I don't have any advisor.

So, this mine gives you access to gold at a cheaper price and then you can resell it to your customers. Is that kind of it?

Yes, honey, that is the deal. I will get it very cheap.

And will you be able to tell the quality by looking at it?

I am buying it for 500k; that is the whole deal.

That's a very interesting business indeed. I'll say my prayers that it works out perfectly.

God bless and give you a good heart.

I will be proud to have you at my side and my hand in yours and our arms around each other.

Yes that will be the moment I have been looking forward to.

Last night, before falling asleep, I laid in bed with three photos of you and your note that came with the flowers. I just thought about how wonderful it is to have you in my life.

Yes and I also do the same, as I have your picture on my screen. Believe me.

I think my new best friend and lover is blind, but they say love is blind!

So when we are together, I will wake up and just watch you sleep. So I can give you a kiss and go back to sleep. And say to myself how lucky I am to have you.

I think you will fall asleep first at night. And I will listen to you breathing. And I will tell you how in love I am with you.

If I could put into words how you make me feel when I think of you, and how much you excite me when I hear your sweet sexy voice.

I live for the day that I can sit next to you and whisper into your ear and tell you that I love you and kiss you ever so lightly but passionately on your lips and to look into your beautiful eyes as you take my breath away.

I live for that first look into your eyes, that first passionate kiss, that first embrace, and that first time that we make love together. I live to spend a lifetime with you as your husband and to grow old with you, loving you for all times from now to eternity.

I am so taken by Tom's words. Wow, this is really incredible. I met this man only 19 days ago, and he is convinced he will marry me.

How did this happen? How do I deserve such love? I have never had anyone say such beautiful, heartfelt things to me.

I am just reading and re-reading your words ...

You cannot propose to me on Hangouts!! LOL

I don't want to lose you for anyone else or anything that anyone has to say about you. I want you to know that I love you from the deepest part of my heart. And those flowers show everything. I just wish that there was another way that we could be together without living so far apart right at the time being.

I won't propose to you on here. But when the time comes, you will see it.

I'm in love with you, I won't lie about that. Even though I am thousands of miles away from you; I am forever by your side.

Tom, 19 days ago, you walked into my life. In that short time, we became attracted to each other, learned about each other, laughed a lot, cried some. You said one day, when I was in Florida, that we were experiencing the wonderful excitement of falling in love. And you were right. I have fallen in love with an incredible man—Tom Miller. A man I have spoken to for 19 days; written to for 19 days. And longed for over 19 days.

Annie, you have imperfections just like everyone else, but that is why I love you. You make me laugh; you make me cry tears of joy. I truly could not live my life without having you to talk to and to confide in. You know more about me than anyone, you know my thoughts, and you know my heart inside and out.

I thank God every day for letting me meet you and for you falling in love with me. Because my love for you is so real. I wish I had family to come and meet you first, I mean my brother or sister, they would have come to you first and tell you (sic). That I am really in love with you.

Before I will even come there and meet you.

I am crying now. Is that how it happens in your family? Someone tells the woman in advance that the man is truly in love with them? That is lovely. That is so touching.

Yes, I will let a family member come to you as (a sign of) respect. I won't hurt you.

That is so beautiful, thoughtful, loving, caring. Thank you, God, for bringing Tom into my life. Thank you for giving me the courage to be vulnerable by entering a site like Match. Thank you for having Tom online at that very moment and connecting us. Thank you for bringing such a kind, warm, loving man into my life. Thank you for giving me the opportunity to love again. Thank you for bringing Tom into my life while my mom is alive so she can meet him, see his goodness, see the happiness in my eyes when I am with him. Thank you, Lord, for giving me another chance to share my life with someone.

Life is so unpredictable. Changes always come along in big or small ways. I don't know what happened that this sudden change has turned my world upside down for the better. I don't know exactly what it is, but it just hit me that there is something really special about you.

Yes, love always comes to those who wait for it and needs (sic) it the most. Because we have all been through some bad moments, and I don't think we will hurt each other again. Because we both know how it feels like to be hurt.

You are a rare combination of so many special things. You are really amazing and (a) hardworking woman, I like it.

You are as well. Hard working, confident, sensitive, loving, gentle, probably amazing in bed, just a good man.

You have got me dreaming about you.

I can't help it, you have become a part of my world and it scares me because I haven't depended on anyone in a long time. I would trust you with everything. I do trust you with everything. I am and I pray to God that you never do anything to make me regret it.

Gosh, I think the same thing. I typed once and erased the following words: don't ever hurt me, don't ever deceive me, don't ever lie to me. I feel like I have opened my heart to you in such a vulnerable way and it is indeed scary.

I don't want you to be scared. I will protect you like an egg. I would always be there in good or bad times. Just let me know.

Thank you. And I am here for you as well. You will never be lonely again.

What do you have to do this morning?

Only work out at some point. And I have a hair and waxing appt at 11:00. Have you had breakfast? Are you packed?

Yes. I have had my nice breakfast and I have repacked. Thanks for asking.

It's the woman's day! The city will be packed!

Yeah and it's already getting packed. LOL

Oh my, Tom alone in DC when a million women have arrived. Be good!

I will miss you, but I will be there soon, so when I arrive, I will move on to Hong Kong and get a hotel.

I don't like just any woman.

OK, let me know when you land. Share your hotel name with me. I will be waiting to know you are safe. And I especially will want to know when you are flying back!

Of course. And I will (sic) like you to order some Chinese food for me. Will you?

Yes, anything!

And do you know some names of different ones?

Hmm, it's been awhile ...

so we will be able to talk about it.

I thought you meant names of hotels.

No, no I meant the food.

The dumplings are the best!!!!

The Chinese food.

Duck's feet, still with feathers!

LOL

Snake, and you get to drink the blood!

you're kidding me.

All of that is mainland China, of course, not Hong Kong.

I won't drink snake blood!

I'll tell you a story about that someday.

Okay. So how long were you in China?

When I lived in Australia, I went to China and HK many times for business. Usually a week at a time.

I can't wait to hear that story from you. It could be scary.

Tell me when you have to go.

I love you, Tom Miller.

Honey, you asked, how I will get the gold home. Can I have it sent to you and keep it in your garage until I return? Can you do that? Because I can't be with it on the plane.

Another shocker of a question. He wants to send the gold to my house? Is he crazy? I don't know about this ...

> You want to store gold in my garage? That's a little risky!

I am not going to store it there.

> LOL

You know I have to ship it and I am not at home to get it.

> OK, what paperwork will I need to pick it up? And how heavy is $500k of gold? I have a bad back!

I think it's about 180kg. I will check that.

> I hope you are insuring it!

Yes, I will do everything, but I want to know it's OK before I get there. And it will be between us.

Yes, I will do the paperwork and I will make sure I have your name on the paperwork if it's needed. So when you pick me up from the airport, I will already meet the buyers and make a deal.

Is that ok, if I have to do it. If not, and it gets to my house, I will get robbed.

No, it can come here. I just need to be here to sign for it. Next week I have a couple of client meetings. Just checking my calendar.

Yes, but I won't do anything without your agreement.

I work from home on Thursday and Friday.

But won't the gold have to clear customs, etc.?

I won't do something that you won't agree on. I am an honest man and I want you to know that. I won't hurt you. Because we all know God answers our prayer. Unless those who don't believe there is God.

Yes the gold has to clear customs and it will come from there to your house. I will just make all the payments. You will just receive it and sign.

But I will know how their things work when I meet them. We haven't done business before.

OK. I can sign for it. Just make sure it is coming into the country legally and all that.

I'm feeling a bit nervous. He's sending the gold to my house? That is just weird. Why wouldn't he just be traveling home with it? I don't think this makes sense.

The gold I was making for you is ready. I wanted to send it to you, but I didn't trust the mail.

Yes I will do that. I promise you.

Yes, I trust you.

I have about three hours before I fly.

And it's a 14-hour flight! Yikes!

You should have booked business class and written it off as a business expense on your taxes.

Honey, I didn't even know I was spending the night.

LOL

He has been my travel agent for a long time, but sometimes we have a fight.

You are a tall man ... maybe the flight won't be full and you can get a row to yourself for more space.

Make sure you give yourself extra time to get to the airport because of the traffic, protesters, etc.

Yeah, but I will walk there.

I thought it was 20 minutes driving?

He is walking from downtown to the airport. That makes no sense at all. That isn't walkable. Now I am confused.

Yes, I told you about 15 mins.

I just feel like walking and looking around a little bit.

eu te amo!

viagem segura

You speak Portuguese?

LOL

Volte para mim

Or did you translate?

Technology is a beautiful thing!

Como você sabia disso?

You want to take me back to my roots huh?

eu sou inteligente

The airlines just called to found(sic) out if I am around and safe. That is nice of them.

Cool! Don't miss that flight!

I won't miss it.

Tom, I'm going to let you get on your way to the airport. I love you. I will miss you. Good luck with your business transaction. Be safe. I know it's three hours, but security will be high with all the big shots in town.

Yes I know, Annie. I will be on my way and enter the shower now.

You are my world, Killer Miller!

Aww

Nice.

You're mushy, I like that.

I like the man running!

Please go shower. Text me when you have boarded, ok? Big kiss! Bye for now, my new best friend and lover, Tom.

I love you!

Bye.

I love you too.

Day 21, January 22

I'm Scared

From: Tom Miller <happysmile4868@gmail.com>
Sent: Sunday, January 22, 2017 4:51 AM
To: anniem@yahoo.com
Subject: Hello Annie

Good morning, Annie. How are you and how are you doing? I haven't get (sic) a mail from you, but I hope all is well with you. I miss you so much. Well I arrived safely in BEIJING this afternoon around 3:25 PM but something terrible happened. I lost my luggage when I got here so I had to wait to track it. I waited so long and they were found later. So I had to continue to HONG KONG where I am going to stay and where the business will take place, which was a 2 hour drive from BEIJING. I got here at 5:15 PM. I am so tired after this long trip. So I don't want to do anything. I just had to have some rest after such a long day. I missed you. So I just connected my laptop so we can chat but you were not on and there was no email for me. So I just hope everything is alright as I can't call now. I am going to rest for a while and I will be having a meeting with some people and a meeting with the lawyer I want to work with, and the managers of the mining company, so I won't be able to talk online till tonight here in China, but I believe it will be morning or noon in the States. I had a long day yesterday. I have been thinking about you every moment. I just want to hug you, but you are some miles away. What I wouldn't do for a hug. Sometimes it's better to put love into hugs than to put it into words. I want to give thanks for all the time we have spent in conversation. It means a lot to me and I am not moved by the masses but rather by brilliance. This feeling just grows as you wrap yourself around my thoughts. I keep you close to my heart and wish I was speaking with you now if even only online. Such is patience when trust is the bond and love is the binding force. I wrap you with a spell of protection. I'm bringing tender kisses to you in my arms and in my dreams.

Your new friend and lover,

Tom

A two-hour drive to Hong Kong? I think he must mean flight. He must be tired.

Hi!!!!!

Hello, Annie

Good morning to you!

Hi! Tell me all about today!

Wow my day has been wonderful, just long.

Everything is under control. They have done the bars for me already, because I spoke with them when I was in DC. I didn't know the flight will (sic) take that long.

Wow! Already! Have you had meetings too today?

Yes, I have had two meetings today.

I even told the driver to take a picture of the bars for me. Wait, maybe you will (sic) like to see how it looks and it's not something you have to be scared off (sic). I will send it to your phone. I don't know if you will get it. One sec.

OK

It's not working on my phone, I will send it here.

Sometimes the network is bad.

So how has your day been?

Did you sleep well? I miss you so, so much.

My day only just started! I woke up, looked for a text from you. Then looked at my email and saw your beautiful note! Now I am in the kitchen making fresh mango orange juice.

I called a girlfriend of mine, Michelle, because her dad was just diagnosed with cancer and I wanted to check in. I was just beginning to tell her about you when you called!

Did you get the picture on your phone(?) I sent it.

They look like boxes of Godiva chocolate!

I love mango and you better leave some for me. I will be with you this weekend or Friday. I will give you my flight information when I have it done.

LOL

Friday is perfect!

So I can't wait to hold you.

Seriously, how are you shipping them?

I will ship them to your place first, because I won't be home when it arrives.

You better insure them!

Yes I will insure them. But, honey, there is one favor I will ask from you. I hope you don't let me down.

Long pause ...

Oh geez, what now? ... I thought all the 'favors' were behind us. What else could he possibly need from me?

Can I ask? I am waiting for your answer.

I guess it's not another iTunes card.

Yes, you can ask. I will do anything as long as it is legal and does not put my life in danger.

Honey, after meeting the lawyer and doing some other stuff, I want you to loan me 7k so I will give it back to you on Monday or after you have picked me up. I will give you an account here so you can transfer it for me.

$7,000!!! Holy crap! He asks like it's five bucks. Why does this seem so easy for him? Oh dear Lord, how do I handle this? ...

Tom, I don't like requests like that. You have to imagine how it sounds on my end. And me sending money to an account in HK? It's just weird.

Honey, it's just the company I am working with, that is why I need this help. I beg you with Gods (sic) name. I am already here.

I can't walk on the street with that kind of money. That is why I want it transferred into an account. This will be the first and last help I am asking from you.

When we are together, I would never ask anything from you.

I know that is not what you like.

I would rather send it to your account in Pittsburgh. And then you can ask your bank to transfer it to HK.

I can't believe I'm even considering this.

I know it's not right to do this, but I think this is the time that I need your support (the) most. I am very different and I am still me, as you know. I am just in a very bad situation now and it can happen to anyone.

And 7K is not a huge amount of money to me, but the situation with the bank freezing my account has made it so, and believe me it can happen to anyone. Could be you or just anyone else. I beg you with Gods (sic) name. Believe me and I won't let you down.

What about my question? I (will) send it to your account and you wire it.

Honey, I can't access my account because they are finding out what happened; remember that? I told you someone had hacked it.

So I even came here with a money order. Please help me.

It's the first and last thing I am asking from you. I beg you with Gods (sic) name. I really need it.

Dear Lord, please protect me in this moment. Ensure me this is a lawful thing I am doing and not getting myself into trouble. I am a good person. $7k is a lot of money to me. Help me to trust this man, Amen (that is my prayer).

Yes, my love, trust me.

And I will be with you (in) the next few days. And I will sell some over there and let you see how it works. I promise.

God knows my heart. And it has to be btw us. Because I am not a needy man.

OK, I will do it. Email to me the wire transfer instructions. If all of this is a big scam, I have no one but myself to blame. But know that I have a really good friend who will help me if this all goes wrong.

God, why do you say that, Annie?

I'm scared.

So you want me to lose after I have come all this way? I know you are scared, but please trust me and believe in God.

I am even crying here.

Me too.

I feel like I have been blessed with you.

And once in a lifetime someone cares about me after it's been a while. God bless you and I would never let you down.

God never thinks bad(ly) of me.

If you will help me, tell me, so I will send the information and you can confirm when you will do it.

OK, I believe you. Yes, I will do it for you. I will go to the bank at 9:00 AM. I should be able to do a transfer before I leave for my client meeting.

The wire transfer needs to have a comment section with your name and the purpose of the transfer.

Purpose of the transfer has to be (a) business payment.

It can be (a) business payment on behalf of Tom Miller or something like that. But your name must be on it.

Okay, so you can't do it from home. What time will you be leaving for the bank?

The company name is on the account and not me.

And I will need a copy of the receipt from you.

I know the company name will be on the account. But when the transfer comes in, they need to know it is from you and not another customer. And it is important to me that the transfer is connected somehow with your name. If I called five friends right now, each one of them would tell me not to do this.

What the hell am I agreeing to!? Why do I trust this man?

Did you say you are going to a university in Philadelphia? Are you going to teach over there? LOL

Yes, a class on business corruption!!!!

Why did he just change the subject?

Honey, when good things are coming your way, no one will know it. But when we disclose something important about our life, why should you share with your friends?

God knows my heart, Annie. I won't be here to hurt you. This is the time I need your help and support (the) most. And I promise you, when we are together, I won't ask anything from you again.

Be completely humble and gentle; be patient, bearing with one another in love. Make every effort to keep the unity of the Spirit through the bond of peace. Ephesians 4:2-3

I won't lie to you for (sic) anything. If you won't help me, I understand.

Please tell me the purpose of the payment and why you only know you need it now, and not before you went to HK.

The purpose for (sic) the money is to add to the shipment payment and the lawyer ...

OK, my friend. I can't do international wires online. I have to do it through the bank in person. E-mail me the instructions and I'll do it tomorrow morning.

God bless you.

And I hope you don't let me down. As I count on you, and also I need to know when the gold arrives. You better not tell anyone. I beg you with Gods (sic) name.

Why does he say not to tell anyone? And why is that little birdie on my shoulder telling me this does not feel right?

God protect me, would be a better prayer.

You will need to confirm the delivery date so I am here to receive it.

I will give you the tracking number and shipping company site, so you can track it. Do you understand?

I will get it by the time you wake up tomorrow or when you send it after, because I will add it to the payment. I trust you and I need you to trust me. God knows my heart and he will protect you.

And do not forget to do good and to share with others, for with such sacrifices God is pleased. Hebrews 13:16. I will always remember what you did for me. And I will speak of it in front of your friends when we get together. And I know it's soon. I will make you proud.

I keep looking at your picture and it keeps me moving.

Are you going to church today?

I took Mom yesterday to church and then to dinner. I will go work out soon. Not sure if you saw my email, but I was thinking of writing a book called *19 Days.* I think I now know the ending. A secret shipment comes to Annie's house. The bad guys (wearing black clothes, of course), follow the truck. They break into her house and murder her and take the boxes. No one finds her for days because she lives alone. Her new love, Tom, is stranded at the airport, as Annie does not show up to pick him up. It will be a best seller!

LOL

But nothing is going to happen to you.

God's protection is on you and I believe you know that.

Do you want me to give you the account information now?

Yes, can you email it so I can print it?

I will send it to your phone.

Can you email instead?

Also, let me know the hotel where you are staying.

Did you get my text?

Yes, but email would be better so I can print it.

Okay hold on a sec

They got me this hotel. And I have the harbour close by, so it won't be a big deal. I see the harbour from my hotel.

Royal Plaza Hotel.

I Google the hotel.

It looks nice online.

Really not that nice LOL.

I then Google the shipping company.

The company you are dealing with has only been in business for about a year and a half.

I hope you trust them.

Yes I trust them and like I told you before, they are working with the Zijin Mining Company.

So I am just buying from them and leave Asia without nobody knowing I am here. Hope you understand me.

We are safe.

OK, it's late there now, right? You probably need some rest. I'm going to work out. If you can email that address to me, that would be great, otherwise I have to re-type it. I have never done a wire transfer with my bank before. My ex did all that. So, I'll text you afterwards when the transaction has been completed and I'll take a photo of the receipt and send to you. Big hug and kiss to my new best friend and lover, Tom. I love you.

OK, honey.

It's 12am here.

I will talk with you when I am awake and be careful. Please email or text me.

Will do, handsome! Good night! Sleep well!

Promise me you won't let me down. And I will send the mail now.

I promise.

God bless you.

And whatever you get from me, one of this (sic) days, I mean it and it's an answer I'll want from you.

I won't say it!

Yeah, let's meet first and make sure I survive all this!

Maybe it will be there before I arrive and it's not the shipment. Surprise lol

Would you please go to bed so I can work on making my body amazing? It's hours and hours of sit-ups!

OK.

Goodnight.

Bye.

Goodnight, handsome. Until tomorrow ...

$7,000. What am I doing? He sounds so sincere. And if he truly is in a jam all the way in Hong Kong, I should help him. If this is all true, he will pay me back. If not, it's an expensive lesson learned.

I don't sleep well that night. The next morning I receive the wire instructions from Tom in an email.

From: Tom Miller <happysmile4868@gmail.com>
Sent: Sunday, January 22, 2017 11:35 AM
To: anniem@yahoo.com
Subject: Hello Annie

BENEFICIARY NAME : HONGKONG TRADING COMPANY LTD

BENEFICIARY ADDRESS : ROOM 1405A, 14/F ... LUCKY CENTRE.

165-171 WANCHAI ROAD, WANCHAI, HONGKONG

TEL: 0086 - 13823570285

BANK NAME : THE INTERNATIONAL BANK OF HONG KONG

BANK ADDRESS : 83 DES VOEUX ROAD, CENTRAL

ACCOUNT NUMBER : 369-174339-883

From: anniem@yahoo.com
Sent: Monday, January 23, 2017 8:30 AM
To: Tom Miller <happysmile4868@gmail.com>
Subject: Re: Hello Annie

Good morning, Tom! You are either sleeping due to jet lag or (are) already busy on your contract. It's 8:15 AM here.

My bank opens at 9:00. I presume there will be someone there who can execute an international wire. I will have to be on my way to my client by 10:00 AM. If there is a problem, I'll have to go back to the bank after my meeting but before 5:00 PM. I'll text you either way.

You just texted me ... so I know you are awake.

I am so looking forward to picking you up at the airport. That will be an important day for us! I will have a sign with your name on it ... just like the professionals! In case you don't recognize me!

I miss you. I feel so connected to you. You have stolen my heart, Mr. Miller.

Cutting this short so I can dash to the bank.

Love,

Annie

I go to my bank and meet with someone who can help me with an international wire. The bank representative has to telephone someone in the wire room. The wire room representative asks to speak to me. She asks how I know Tom Miller. She asks the nature of the wire. She tells me that once the wire is executed, she won't be able to get the money back. I tell her I understand and say it is fine to send the wire. The bank initiates the wire and gives me a receipt. When back in my car, I take a picture of the receipt and text it to Tom so he has confirmation of the wire transfer. I'm still feeling uncertain about all this. But it's done.

Day 22, January 23

I Need a Gun

From: Tom Miller <happysmile4868@gmail.com>
Sent: Monday January 23, 2017 6:54 AM
To: anniem@yahoo.com
Subject: Good morning

You my love,

A very good morning to you. You are the essence and charm of my life. You mean music to my ears, concern to my heart and add value to my life. You are worthy of all love and praise from the bottom of my heart.

I have never been lucky much in life and the world has not been so loving and caring to me. But your presence has brought fragrance to my life and I have started loving life as never before. You have added a meaning to my life. It has never been like this before.

You are the loving companion I always wanted and adored in my life. You are the most beautiful woman on earth and any man would love being with you. I appreciate you have chosen me.

We will always be with each other in every mode of life, in all ups and downs and in all untrodden paths of life. I promise to give you the life you always dreamt of. We will surely make the best couple on earth. We will have several adventures of (sic) life together and (I) even promise you the most wonderful intimate time. You too will remember me always. I love you more than any other woman on earth since I don't have any family left and I will say you are my family now and I hope you will accept me.

I want you to promise being (sic) with me always. I cannot survive without you now. You are the one whom I trust and with whom I can share the most loving and most bitter experiences of life. I long for the time you will be in my arms and we will spend hours and days together.

The most important thing is that when one has a loving friend like you becoming a life partner (sic), what can be greater than that(?) You are the one who can understand me, know me, be with me, help me, love me.

You will soon realize how strongly I talk from the bottom of my heart. I promise to share all the burdens of life together and have a wonderful time together. I promise to be a good and responsible partner and (the) best father. Hope you have the same committed attitude towards me. Love you, sweetheart.

I have so much to offer you and I have been holding the feelings deep inside my heart. I have tried to open up a little, but there is a lot more in the pool for you.

Your eyes reveal the feelings from the bottom of your heart though you are always shy to speak it out. You can take your own time to order your words.

Love you,

Tom

> Good morning, handsome!

Good morning, beautiful.

How are you and how was your night?

It's good to be the person to tell you goodnight and also wish you good morning. I want to sleep next to you and wake up with you as well.

> LOL, you ask how my night was, but remember I was just having my day while YOU slept!

> Which side of the bed do you prefer?

I am lost. I prefer the front of the bed. I have to protect my woman.

> Side closest to the door?

I thought I was still in the States! But I wanted to tell you, Pittsburgh is more beautiful than this side of Hong Kong. Do you believe that?

Of course we will sleep on the same bed, but the side closest to the bed.

Let me ask the question a different way. If we are laying in the same bed, both on our backs, are you on the right side or the left side?

Okay it will depend on the gate, but I like the front anytime.

What the F are you talking about? LOL

Sorry, depends on where the door is facing but, I want you to see me first, when you open our room door.

OK, in my house, that puts you on the left side, which is perfect! Because I always sleep on the right side!

Yes, I was trying to say that.

Actually, I said that entirely wrong. That puts you on the right side, and me on the left. You'll see what I mean when you are here.

Look at the bed photo you sent me. I would like to sleep on the side where there was (sic) no pillow.

Perfect! That is your side!

But I will give you a pillow, because I am nice.

LOL. I know you will treat me nice because I have been laughing all along.

So what are your plans today?

I have a meeting at noontime, and there is one more box I need to get.

I am even already looking for buyers for some of it. So don't worry, this year will be our year!

I wanted to tell you, if you would like me to talk with Jack so I can show him how my business works, so I can leave it to him someday. I am happy to. But don't ask him now, unless I see him myself. Just asking, if I make sense.

You certainly can ask him. It's hard to say if this will be of interest to him. Since I'm living till at least 96, you can leave it to me! LOL

Ha, but we will be living together. Trust me, he will always work for it and the most important thing is I will leave him with a lot of information. I would like our family to have a small jewelry store, and you can take care of it when you are not working anymore. Like I told you, it's my last business trip. I need to enjoy life. Life is too short.

I'm all for enjoying life! Sign me up!

Yes, and you have already been signed up. I need you by my side. And I want you to be true to me. I need someone like you.

Yeah, I'm a pretty good catch!

I believe you are happy, like I am.

I will give you a big hug that you will never expect. I feel like I have known you forever.

It's weird, isn't it? I feel the same way. And now we have known each other for just 20 days. I feel very fortunate to have you in my life. I so look forward to your hug, to fall asleep in your arms, to have a meal together, to make love.

Yes, Annie. I know and I know God has his hands on us.

My neighbor was right. She said the universe wanted me to have the time in FL alone, and that gave us the chance to get to know each other.

Every day I feel so lonely, seeing my friends and business clients going out with their lovers to meetings and dinner. I will be lucky to go with you.

Do you have any food allergies?

You will see me in a tuxedo and I will love to see you dress sexy and lovely.

Oh, I can't wait! I love to dress up! I have some really sexy black dresses.

Oh well, I just don't eat normal stuff.

Back to dressing up for a second. I think when I see you in a tux, you will take my breath away!

Oh well, then it will happen for sure.

I have a lot of tuxes.

You have more than one?

Will you be my Valentine?

Yeah, I have more than one.

Yes, I will be your Valentine.

Good

It's at this point that I decide to mail a Valentine to Tom's house so that he receives it when he gets home from Asia. I want it to be a surprise!

Have you eaten dinner?

Yes, made a nice salad with roasted chicken.

Yummy

Let me know when you need to leave.

And where is mine?

Ha

Oh it's 10:16 AM.

America is more beautiful then (sic) China, believe it or not.

But isn't it wonderful to be in HK? I always loved it there!

It's weird that he refers to China this way, as Hong Kong and China are not the same.

Oh. Yes it's beautiful in HK, but the language LOL

It's tough; the intonation is so hard. Do you have to have a translator or is (the) business in English?

Yes, I need to have one.

So what are you thinking about your return to the States(?) You may arrive Friday, and when do you want to go back to Pittsburgh?

I do swear that I will always be there for you. I will give you anything and everything and I will always care. Through weakness and strength, happiness and sorrow, for better or worse, I will love you with every beat of my heart! You are the love of my life and I am glad that I picked you to fall in love with. I thank God every time I go to sleep. And I hope you love me and won't let me down.

I will go to Pittsburgh in 4-5 days, even if you don't want to accept me in your house for that long. Maybe you would like to go to work and can't leave me with (sic) your house. But I have been working for a long time for this moment in my life. I haven't had a break, so like I told you it's my last trip and I need some time off and (to) make some good sales.

To go back to Pittsburgh together, we would have to travel on a Friday, like Feb 3rd. I have a client lunch that day, so we could leave after that.

I will definitely have to work that week. Some days at home, some days with a client. But hey, your 'boxes' are more valuable than anything I own! So no worries for you to be here.

I think the gold bars could be worth around eight point six million. It's a secret.

$8.6MM???? Wow, that is amazing. He can definitely take care of me with that type of money. I may have hit the lottery with Mr. Miller!

Tom, I am speechless!!!

Yeah, and I couldn't laugh when I saw the gold.

But I don't have to keep it with me, so it's still with them.

We will take it from the warehouse to the shipping company. So everything will be done there.

I don't have a security system in my house. Now I'm nervous. What will the shipping company think they are delivering?

And the boxes will be way too heavy for me to move (like to the basement to hide them).

It won't be long. I will have the buyer as soon as I get there.

No, don't worry about security. Nobody knows you are having something like that delivered.

OK ... I hope you get here soon!

Yes, I will get there soon. I need to deal with a few things here first. And it can't be shipped with a passenger plane.

If I were you ... I'd be on that cargo plane sitting right on top of the boxes! Ha

So I have to ship it with a company who does that job. And they are a trusted company. I know you are alone and I won't put your life in (sic) risk. Never in my life.

I think I'm going to buy a gun.

Why should you buy a gun? LOL

For protection!

Have you told anyone that something like this is coming to your house? Please tell me?

Be honest.

NO WAY!

How can two people fall in love without having seen each other in person? Without having shared time together? Without having had a meal together? Without having kissed each other? This is new territory for me.

Remind me, how long were you on Match before meeting me?

The 'no way' meant I have not said a single thing to anybody.

I lose the Hangouts signal.

Hello, babe

Hey!

I was just looking at your picture while I waited; the one of you in your workout room, shorts only.

LOL

Probably socks too!

Lol

Us meeting is something that has to happen.

You are funny!

I'm funny? Didn't you tell that you wear socks to bed? But let's be clear: when you're in my bed, you won't have anything on you but me!

Yes, I won't have anything.

You are making me laugh.

What would you like to do when you get here? Would you like to go out to dinner? Have me make you something here? Any preference?

Of course, you'll need to meet my mom while you are here. Are you brave enough to meet Mary?

Yes, I would like to be with you while making dinner for me or whatever you prefer.

Yes, I would like that.

I think it would be better if your family met me at your house and had dinner with us. While we get to know each other and laugh a bit.

Well first, it will be just you and me. I want us to have time together!

I want you to be comfortable in my home. Mi casa, su casa.

Oh, OK.

That is a good idea.

So you would like us to have dinner somewhere nice?

No, I think we should have dinner here, at my house.

That will be special. I would like to see you in (a) white top walking around the house.

I won't hide my feelings from you and remember I have had that dream about you.

I would never let you down.

I am so glad that you are not the kind of woman that would cheat on me and you should know that I would NEVER cheat on you. I love you.

White top? Like a t-shirt, or button down, or your shirt? Yes, I remember that dream. I have re-read it many times.

I will be faithful to you till the end of time.

Yes, like a T-shirt.

Bra or no bra?

Of course no bra.

You got it! I was trying to think of what to wear when I pick you up. Now I know!

I thought it was so cute the first time you said I love you because I know you were trying so hard to let it out, but you weren't sure when would be a good time it say it.

You are soooo right.

Our 'goodbyes' online seemed like something was missing before that. It seemed so right, so natural to tell you I loved you.

I hope we last a lifetime because I want to have a family with you. I seriously think that you would be a great mother and a great wife and friend to me. If you think of us, just remember to let our love burn! I love you with all my heart and I miss you so much right now.

I think about you all the time. I miss you so much. I am in love with you, Mr. Miller. I hope we have many, many years together, God willing.

Honey, the driver just came here. So I will be leaving to the warehouse. I would (sic) let you know when I am back. Sometimes the connection is bad.

Bye, my love.

Day 23, January 24

The Ring

> Good morning, handsome!

> Good morning.

> Are you out of your shower now?

> Yup doing hair, makeup, the routine. How was the warehouse visit?

> The warehouse visit was cool, but like I told you, I don't like it when I can't speak the language and I have to use a translator.

> I was at the warehouse with the lawyer to check if everything is (sic) in order because I have to see what is going on. So far I like how the business is going on. But I have you on my mind often. And it makes my day really easy and awesome.

> What are you doing tonight? Have you already had dinner? Have you walked around downtown HK?

You know I like sports, so I told the driver to take me to the Wan Chai Sports Ground, so I went to look around.

But I will go to the Victoria Harbour in the morning. So I will keep you updated.

In HK the Peak is nice to do in the evening. Good views if the air is clear. In HK, it's mostly people watching and shopping.

Just fascinating to walk around.

How has the food been?

The food has been nice, believe me. When I look into (sic) their menu, I choose something different. I got your text.

I haven't been to the bank yet as I was very sleepy when I woke up. I believe I have been working for a long time so I

had to tell the driver to give me time to rest. I needed to rest my body a little bit.

No worries. I am sure the transfer went thru. It is hard to travel to Asia. It's a tough adjustment for the body. How did the meeting go with the shipping company?

I have an appointment with the shipping company agent at 3:15 PM

Did you make it to any of the sites?

Yes, I went to the jade market.

It was awesome

I've been there! It is really interesting.

Yes, it was very lively and interesting as I saw a lot of short people!

Oh my goodness.

Did they all stare at you because you are a giant compared to them?

Yes a lot of them were staring at me. And they knew I was new in town.

Yes, they saw I was new in town, because I was asking the tour guide, 'Hey what is this and that?' What would you like from here?

You!

And definitely you.

And positively you.

Nothing more.

Aww, thanks so much.

And 3 three heavy boxes of 'Godiva chocolate boxes'!

Do you understand?

I just want your trip to be a success.

Yes,

I understand that.

Yes I want the same thing as well.

Perhaps today you will learn more about when you can come back?

I tried the spaghetti here last night!

Oh? How was it?

It was yummy, but the chopsticks were a challenge.

LOL

I hope you weren't wearing a white shirt!

I just thought I will try the noodles and the tour guide helped me to do that. So pray for me.

Have you tried dumplings?

No I haven't

That is a must!

Okay I will order this at lunch today and I will tell you.

Have you gone anywhere else on tour?

No I haven't gone anywhere as I don't know anywhere over here. Like I told you. I always travel for business.

If we were to be together for this trip, then we would have a lot to do.

That's for sure! Next time!

But they like smoking on the street too much and I hate that.

Ugh! I forgot about that.

Smoking is not good for human health.

I agree! I should warn you that Jack smokes. I know he will quit soon, but I guess not while he is sick.

What does he smoke?

Weed or what?

No, no,

cigarettes.

Okay he better stop if he wants to be 95 years. LOL

You're right! But my dad smoked and lived to 91!

I guess his life was cut short!

LOL

It's also how you look after yourself. I have been rereading your mail over and over again. I like it a lot.

And I want you to know that you have every reason to believe that we will continue to grow together as a couple, as partners, as best friends, as lovers. And a lot more!

I was wondering if you had read it and what you were thinking. Thanks for commenting. I don't use the same words as you at the moment, but my heart is with you.

Thanks for being there for me. And I would (sic) always be there with you in good or bad times.

Me as well. As much as I think we will have some amazing, happy, loving, exciting, and adventurous times, I know there will be moments of sadness. And I am so glad I have you to be by my side.

Words can no longer describe it, but rather it is a feeling and emotion that we have for each other.

I'm so glad to hear your (sic) say that. Then I am off the hook in trying to write something as poetic as you! Ha

You have always had the key to my heart, and (having) you inside my heart has made me more than I can (sic) ever be. Though the sea separates us till that special day, I know we take each breath and every beat of our hearts together.

I have saved up all my words and love for that special someone, so I am not surprised for (sic) feeling this way.

I am soooo fortunate to be that woman. You have so much love to give. I will drown (in a good way) in your love, words, emotion, and attention.

And Tom, I will not let you down. I will continue to be here for you. I want to fill that void you have had in your heart for so long. I want to show you that the universe has love waiting for you. I want you to feel part of a family again.

Thank you so much.

I love you.

I love you too, Annie.

And I thank the universe for you.

I'm sad that I will not meet your parents. But perhaps you can share their picture with me someday and tell me more about them. To bring them to life for me.

I hope you know how much you really mean to me.

Yes I miss them so much. To be honest, I know they are happy for me now, since they see my heart full of happiness.

I would love to share stories of them with you, and we will go to my basement to look at pictures of them together. And we will be laughing.

You are one in a million, baby. Te amo demais!

I can't wait! I think they were sitting next to me on my sofa the night I went on Match. And their voices were the ones saying, 'Hit send; send that profile. Tom is waiting for you.'

Te amo demais!!!

You are extraordinary!

You are making me laugh again! I will visit Ngong Ping 360 when I am less busy.

I'll have to look that up.

Yes the driver told me about it. I would love to go there and have a look around.

It says online that the cable car is not operating. They are doing a rope replacement project. So make sure there are other things to do. I just Googled it.

Really?

I will talk with the driver when he is here.

Sounds good. Have you taken any photos with your phone? You should send me a selfie in Hong Kong!

Yes I have been. The network is not working, because they told me I won't get all the access here.

OK, you can share them with me when you get here.

I forgot to ask, what ring size do you wear?

Oh my goodness! Ring size? He is getting a ring for me? This is unbelievable!

Big feet, big fingers!

7 on the left … 7+ on the right. What shirt size do you wear?

Oh gosh, I got one for you for a surprise, but I shouldn't have told you. But I got a 6.

I am so sorry. I will try to stop it if it's not too late.

I wanted to ask you to wait for me till I get back, so I will make you my wife. So that was the meaning of the ring coming to you. And I mean I love you and I would show you a lot of unexpected love. Something that you had always dreamed of.

What? He mailed a ring to me? Jewelry is always a winner. But a ring? Well, let's see if and when it arrives. I'm suspicious again.

So you have sent this to me? You are full of surprises! Oh my, I sure hope you love me as much in person as you do online!!!

Well, I feel like I have known you forever.

I know, it's crazy! Me as well.

Yes I sent it to you. I had wanted to ask about what size ring you wear.

Gosh, I hope you are not disappointed when we finally meet. Now I'm getting nervous!

I'll squish my finger into it and then it will never come off!

LOL. But it's size 6, so I have to call it back unless it's too late to do that.

I will now fall asleep with a huge smile on my face and dream of you, of us, and you probably need to get some dumplings! Tomorrow I have to get up really early. I'll definitely ring you first thing, but I'll have to get ready for work straight away. I have another two-hour drive to do and an all-day meeting. I love talking to you ... I wish I could just keep talking through the night. I love you, Tom Miller.

I feared failure until I realized that I only fail when I don't try. So I don't give up on anything I do. And I am glad we met.

I love you too, Annie.

That is a great saying.

Are you going back to the university tomorrow? Why do you have to drive another two hours?

I messed up. I should have stayed overnight. I'm going to another client, and they are close to today's. I thought the meeting started at 10:30, but it starts at 8:30 AM. Ugh

Oh. Before we sign off, I need you to know that I'll be emailing a form to you for (your) signature.

What kind of form?

It's a transfer of title form.

> Why do I need to sign that?

I'm getting frustrated with Tom. I don't want the gold to be in my name. Why is that necessary? I am not purchasing it. This just gets weirder every day.

Honey, for the gold to be shipped to your house, customs will want to see your name on the documents.

> Tom, I'm not comfortable with this. I agreed to have everything shipped to me for your convenience, but I don't want this to have my name on it. That could have all kinds of tax and legal implications for me.

> It's getting late. I need to get to bed. Let me think about it.

Babe, I don't understand what you are worried about. I need your name on the document so it can be shipped. If you don't agree to do this, the transaction falls apart. Please, don't get so worried.

> Tom, I'll think about it. I have to go now. Good night.

Ok, Annie, please trust me. I love you. Good night.

Day 24, January 25

The Second Ask

From: anniem@yahoo.com
Sent: Wednesday, January 25, 2017 11:50 AM
To: Tom Miller <happysmile4868@gmail.com>
Subject: Re: Document

Hey handsome,

So sorry the time difference complicates our ability to communicate, besides my work schedule. Please email the document to me today so I can print, sign and return (it) straight away. I'll be limited in what I can do when I get to the office Wednesday. I'd rather take care of it from home. If you need anything when it's my evening, just call me, regardless of the hour.

Thank you for your patience and understanding during all this! I can tell from the tone in your message that I'm frustrating you. So looking forward to your return!

Love

Annie

From: Tom Miller <happysmile4868@gmail.com>
Sent: Wednesday, January 25, 2017 12:20 AM
To: anniem@yahoo.com
Subject: Document

Hello, I have all the time in the world for you. Never use that word again– frustrating. You are never frustrating me. I am happy to have you as a woman and as a person. I know it's not easy when you are alone and trying to make others understand you. I would (sic) let you know as soon as I get the document and I even think it's a good idea to do everything at home. So don't worry, if you have to even go to work and come back and sign it. I am ok. So just take care of whatever you are doing. I love you so so much. I have decided that I am definitely, hopelessly in love with you. What made me realize this is not so much that I think about you all the time, though I do. It was how I think about you. Not only do I think about how much I love you, but why, how much, and mostly do I deserve to be loved by you. What have I done to deserve this? And that is another thing I was thinking. I think that we are so right for each other. Some might want to argue this, but I have a few examples for those poor misguided souls. Your smile is like a world famous painting. All of this tells me one thing: our love is real. So get home and let's talk soon. I love your voice.

Love

Tom

Later that day, I get an email from Tom with a selfie of himself in Hong Kong and the transfer of title form. The picture shows him standing in a street which appears to be Hong Kong. There is something strange about the photo. I can't put my finger on it. I print off the title transfer document. It appears pretty official, but what do I know?

That evening, Tom pings me on Hangouts...

Hello honey, I am here.

Have you eaten something first?

No, (I'm) not really hungry.

How was your day? You sound tired?

Are you okay?

Not really ...

This whole transaction thing has me worried, upset, concerned, etc.

You sound so lovely when we text one moment, and then you sound almost angry the next.

What transaction?

No I am not upset with you. Why should you say that? Did you read my mail?

Yes, I read it.

Why are you upset with me? What have I done?

What's going on, tell me?

Give me a chance. I'm typing now.

The little voice in my head says to me, 'What the F are you doing, Annie?'

I'm still typing …

I just sent $7k to someone that I hardly know. Yes, we asked each other a million questions. We have hardly spoken on the phone. The line is always terrible. Now I'm going to receive property for you that is worth a gazillion dollars. You talk about wanting me as your wife, but goodness, you haven't even met me. Of course you will say, Trust me, God knows my heart, etc. But this is all almost surreal and I'm worried I have gotten myself involved in something that is not right, meaning your purchase. So all this has my stomach (tied) in a knot. I can't sleep, I'm worried. And I think I'm being a stupid, gullible woman. I would have told my girlfriend(s) they were nuts if they were doing what I am doing. So that's what's wrong. Thank you for waiting.

I am sorry for coming into your life.

I don't know what I have done to you. We hardly speak on the phone because I am here and the connection is not the same. You know it.

Can I ask a question and then ask a favor?

Yes ask me whatever you want but just remember that whatever happens, not all friends wish you happiness.

I haven't shared our story with my friends. They only know I met an amazing man named Tom.

So why won't you wait and let us meet?

I know it's not easy for you. I know how happy and fearful you are at the same time. But remember things do happen for a reason. And that means you never meant what you said to me.

Love me without restriction, trust me without fear, want me without demand and accept me for who I am. If you can't do this then you have to let go.

Tom, if you read my note above, I'm just sharing what is bothering me.

Just calm down.

I'm actually pretty calm, believe it or not. I'm sad and feel sick.

I was never upset with you. Maybe I was not happy because I couldn't hear your voice.

Anytime I try to love again or try to build a relationship something has to happen. If you don't want me anymore, just tell me.

SHIT! I didn't say that!

I would (sic) never date again, I swear to you. Why should I always feel alone?

God, what have I done wrong(?)

I didn't meant (sic) to sound the way I did in my message for you to feel that way. I love you and even though we haven't met, my love for you is real.

Can I ask my question and my favor?

Yes anything.

Here's my question: will you swear to me that your purchase is totally legal? That you are not getting me involved in something that I need to fear or worry about(?) That when your Godiva chocolate arrives, I'm not going to get arrested(?)

I swear with my life and my mum's death that I would never plan evil against you.

Everything I work with is legal.

Thank you. And now for my favor.

I want to meet. I so want to meet. But please give me and us some time to get to know each other more before taking it to the next level. You are a very open person, and I admire that. But sometimes I chuckle when I think about the fact that you wouldn't speak to me on the phone until we texted a certain amount, and now you are talking about being life partners. For me, there is another step somewhere. LOL

Honey, if you want to talk on the phone and stop talking here, I agree with that. But I don't want to disturb you.

I do want to talk more, but the connection is always crappy and then it gets frustrating (sorry that word again) when we can't hear each other.

Believe me, I am always ready to talk on the phone.

It's not just about the phone, silly! I just want to make sure we take the time to get to really know each other before you think about putting a ring on my finger! I really want to meet you and spend time face to face, in person, alone and with others.

Yes, that is why I called it back. Maybe it was because I feel so much for you.

I follow my heart, and I know my heart knows what I want.

No, you called it back because it was the wrong size!

Really, he now says he canceled the shipment of the ring because we were moving too fast? That is a bunch of crap. There probably was not a ring to begin with. Ugh...

Always pray to have eyes that see the best in people, a heart that forgives the worst, a mind that forgets the bad, and a soul that never loses faith in God.

Ha! I said I would squeeze it on my fat fingers!

LOL

You know, that is quite beautiful, what you just wrote. I do try to be that person.

Honey, I will get my flight information ready and send it to you. Because I want to arrive on Saturday.

When do my gold boxes arrive?

Anne, I need to ship out (the) gold boxes today, but I can't because of the change of ownership. It will come with other cargo, so maybe two days express.

Are you getting your paperwork today? The time difference confuses me.

Yes, honey, the change of ownership is going to cost me, so I wanted to ask if you will help me? So I know I owe you (already). I will give it all back as soon as you pick me up and we meet the buyers. If not I can't ship it out and my visa is not a long stay.

Long pause.

I'm sorry, I just fainted.

Gosh, fainted, I am serious. Stop doing that. I know I owe you. I will pay you back and you know that.

Are you yelling at me???

If you don't want to help me, it's OK.

No, no, I am not yelling at you.

I want to get out of here.

Do you have a good idea of all (the) remaining costs?

I was in a bit of a hurry to come here. Please. I will pay you back with interest.

Just get me at the airport this weekend and let's sort things out before going home. Please.

Let me get this done and come home. And what did you mean by (the) remaining costs?

The business transaction has had a lot of unexpected costs, that's all.

I will pay you back with one gold bar transaction when I come home.

What will I do with that? Lol

I said, we will meet a buyer as soon as you get me at the airport.

So we will sell it before going anywhere you will take me.

Now I definitely think I am going to be murdered.

At that moment, I will be yours. I won't talk about anything else again.

God, please stop that, OK?

Why would you joke about such a thing? I won't murder even a cat.

Not you! The buyer!

We will meet him after you pick me up from the airport. We will disclose it on the phone.

I will give you the box code, so when you unlock one, you will take one bar out and bring it with you to the airport.

Holy crap!!!!

What? Is he kidding? I'm going to bring a bar of gold to the airport and he is going to get cash for it from a buyer that day? That is crazy!

You're always scared of something. Who knows you have the gold unless you have told someone(?) So why should you be afraid?

This is just not my world. I'm a simple consultant who does organization design work.

LOL

Thank you for laughing.

You are bringing it to me. I will make the business.

So you will just stay in your car.

I guess YOU really trust ME! I'm the one with all the Godiva in my house!!!

Yes I trust you, because I have no right not to. I believe you won't hurt me.

A new house in the south of France. Maybe two new houses, a jag, a big diamond ring. Life is good!

Please can you share with me what was the unexpected costs and if you will help me do the change of ownership, so I can tell the two lawyers and the three Hong Kong court judges so they can start working on my documents?

How much is it?

I ask because I don't keep a lot of cash in my account.

Oh so what are we going to do?

You don't keep it in your account, so where do you keep it, in a safe house? LOL

I invest it, silly!

I need $13k for the documents and the payment of the high court judges and $2k for my ticket. Since I am short.

Tom, I don't have 15k in my account!!!!

Oh my god! He just asked me for $15,000. This cannot be happening. Annie, you know this isn't right. Just listen to the little voice in your head.

How much in total can you help me with and I will see what I can do. Please.

So when I get home on the weekend, I will pay you and (you can) put it back where you took it from.

I can't sell off investments. I can only work with what is in my bank account. I thought you were going to say another $2 or $3k. $15k? There's no way, honey.

Honey, so that means you can't help me?

I really can't. I don't keep that level of cash.

Yes and I am asking, how much can you help me with, so I will talk with them and see what to do (sic). Not even half of it?

Maybe $5? I'm cutting it close. Let me check what bills are clearing.

I'm stalling. I want to believe him. I want to give him the benefit of the doubt. I want him to be real.

Honey, try and (sic) do 8k and I will sell my Rolex watch. If not I won't get money for my ticket as well. Please and I will pay you back when I am home. I promise.

I hope your travel agent can handle your ticket again. I know you are in a jam. I wish you had known about these costs in advance.

What kind of businessman goes to Hong Kong and doesn't know the extent of the fees for the transaction?

You have already helped me and it's you who has invested with me here as well. If things go as planned, I will give you 10%. And don't turn it down.

Gosh, it's not that.

Can they invoice you? Can you give them a credit card? What are your options?

Honey, just 8k and I will take care of the rest, OK? Please.

How would I even get this to you?

Can't you transfer it?

You can wire it of course.

Long pause.

Did you stop talking to me?

No, I'm here. I was actually going to ring you at your hotel to talk through it.

What is your room number?

You can't call me on (the) phone, I told you, this (sic) people gave me the hotel and nobody knows I am there. So you want them to track me now? Gosh.

No, I just wanted a land line for greater reception.

I will call you, I think it will work. So please don't put my life in danger.

> I would never do that!

I don't know anyone here, if something should happen to me and someone knows this American man is in this room number (sic). That could be a problem for me.

Each day, the driver just walks me up to my room and then stays with me for a while and leaves. And that is what we have been doing since I came.

> I'll call you.

Phone conversation:

Tom: Hi my love

Annie: Hey there

Tom: I am worried that you don't trust me.

Annie: Doesn't it seem strange to you that you continue to ask me for money?

Tom: I don't have anyone else to help me. You know my bank account is frozen. I can't use a credit card for these expenses. You have to believe me. I didn't expect to have the extra fees.

Annie: I called the hotel in Hong Kong.

Tom: What? Are you trying to put my life in danger?

Annie: They had no record of a Tom Miller there.

Tom: Annie, the hotel is not in my name. It's in the name of the people I am working with. I told you I can't have people know I am here. Gosh, do you want me to get hurt?

Annie: No, I just want some reassurance that all of this is legit. You know, I was looking at the picture you sent.

Tom: Yes, I had my driver take it of me.

Annie: I noticed that something looked really familiar about your face.

Tom: What do you mean?

Annie: Did you cut and paste your face onto that picture?

Tom: What? What are you talking about?

Annie: Your face is almost identical to the photo you sent me from the concert a couple (of) weeks ago. Never mind.

Tom: Why don't you trust me? I love you, Annie.

Annie: I want to believe you. I'm just getting really nervous about all this.

Tom: These are the last fees for the court here and then the gold can be shipped and I can fly home to be with you. Please, Annie, help me this last time.

Annie: OK, I'll see what I can do.

I do have the money in my account. I talk myself into making this last transfer. After all, the deal will then be done and Tom will fly to Philly to meet me! I so want all this to work out. I want this 'dream' to come true. I want Tom to be all that I imagine he is. And he'll pay me back and all this worrying will be for nothing. He needs me right now. I believe in him.

I make the second wire transfer to the same account as before. Again, the person in the wire transfer room asks to speak to me. She warns me about sending the money. She asks if I really know this person. I'm annoyed she is asking so many questions … and that darn little voice in my head is telling me not to do this. But I ignore all the signs and bank warnings and send the wire transfer. As before, I text a copy of the receipt to Tom. I've now invested $15,000 in this relationship.

Later that day, I get an email from the shipping company that the gold has been loaded and is on its way to the US. I am sooo relieved. Phew! This was all a real transaction. All that worrying for nothing. I send a short email to Tom to let him know of (sic) the notice I received from the shipping company. I am sure he has received the same (message).

I can now relax and stop worrying. I feel the anxiety leave my body. And now all I think about is meeting Tom at the airport this weekend. Finally, we will meet in person. I have really fallen for this man.

Day 25, January 26

The Deal is Done

From: Tom Miller <happysmile4868@gmail.com>
Sent: Thursday, January 26, 2017 4:08 AM
To: anniem@yahoo.com
Subject: Reflection

Dear Annie

When I saw you for the first time, I knew I had found someone wonderful. And ever since then, all I have wanted is to be with you. Seeing you happy brightens my day and makes me think I am doing the right things. You are special and I hope you are having a blessed and wonderful day. I love you so much and I mean every word I say to you. Also about my picture, I don't know what you mean about cut and paste; explain to me. I am honest and try to make (sic) my best for you to understand me.

You have the most loving and forgiving heart I have ever known and I can assure you that you will remain the center of attention for me. I will do everything in my capacity to keep you happy. Our love will be an everlasting friendship and soul mate (sic) because two inseparable souls cannot live in isolation. The day I discover you in (my) arms, that will be the happiest day of my life. And I know it will be soon. I look forward to that. I am not fully awake. I got a mail from the shipping company. So I thought I will get back to them and saw your mail. Did you get any mail from them yourself? I will wake up soon and talk with you. I love you and know that you are a wanted person now.

Thank you for being there, at least in my mind and heart.

Yours,

Tom

Hello Honey,

I have been (sic) to the shipping company, when I woke, because I got an email from them. So I wanted to make sure everything is in order.

You may have seen my follow up email that I did get a confirmation from the shipping company.

Seems things have already left HK.

Yes I saw your mail

Yes and I am finally happy and blessed to have you.

Thank you for your email early (during) your morning. It was beautiful, as usual.

Glad that you like it.

I think you should consider being a writer when you retire.

Really. Maybe it's because I have learned a lot of things on my own.

Maybe. But you certainly have a beautiful way of expressing yourself.

I have a question ...

Anytime!

So, how comfortable are you sleeping in a waterbed?

Well, I have tried it only once, but I liked it.

Good, cause that's what I have. I have always had a waterbed. I find it really healthy for my back.

Awesome. I like it.

So what are you wearing tonight?

A T-shirt and black panties.

Aww, I would love to see it.

Just take a picture for me. Stand in (front of) the mirror.

Nope, you have to wait till you get here. No photos. I am going to make you suffer.

Hmmm

Question, when do you fly home?

I will know tomorrow, when I wake up, because I have to see the gold bars leave the port. Were you able to track it?

Let me check the shipment now ... BRB.

Still showing as having been picked up at Victoria Harbor.

Destination: 18.00 on 1/30, Philly Airport, in the name of Annie St. Clair only. Not to be given to some guy named Tom.

I don't know about where it will move next, but I believe the shipping company knows what they are doing.

HAHAHA

Trust me, baby!

Honey, I want us to look for the ticket pricing together and see what date is good for me to fly back. So can we do that now?

Sure. I was looking earlier and saw 1200 on Expedia for economy. Tell me what site you are going to.

So what airline do you like the most?

No preference. I'm a price shopper.

Oh. Okay.

Let's check on British Airways.

I do like Singapore Airlines the best.

britishairways.com

I will check the Singapore (site) as well.

I'm doing BA, HK to Philly.

Yeah, just the price and let's see.

Hmmm ... Why is it showing in HK dollars???

Because you are checking from HK LOL. Business class is $9,000! Yikes!

Yes, I think so, because I got 74430 HK dollars.

Economy is USD 1300.

Yup, I found the currency converter.

Qatar Airways is $1200 on Expedia.

I want the business class

I see American Airlines also for 1200 USD.

Ok, let me look at that.

This is better. I'm seeing $3600 on Expedia; American Airlines, 1 stop.

I'm going to look at American.com and compare.

Also $3600 if I look at AA's site for Business Class

Yes I think it's better.

I just checked AA. It's the same price.

Which date did you choose?

28th

Unless you think you're getting out today?

But, honey, what are we going to do? How can I get the funds?

I can put it on a credit card. I'll need your passport number, full name as it appears on your passport, date of birth. I guess I know that - 4/25/63?

Oh boy, does he really want me to pay for this? OK, if that is the case, I am going to get all his personal details. With his passport info, I'll be able to confirm he is who he says he is. Am I really questioning that again? I thought I was in a better place?

Yeah, but I wanted to walk into the office and buy my ticket and make a few shopping (sic) from HK. I need to get something home. So I wanted you to come up with something like 5k for me. Because you know if you have to travel out of here, you need to have money in your pocket as a rule. I owe you and I know. I will pay you back by Monday, if I get home on Sunday.

I'd only be able to do it by purchasing it on my card. My account is depleted.

Honey, please, there has to be a way. Because I have to choose a good time to fly, if I have some things to do. Please.

Tom, I'm telling you. I have no way. I have taken $15k out of my account already. I don't have any options. Please understand. That is why I couldn't pay you any more the other day.

He's actually asking for more cash? Annie, what is wrong with you? He is so scamming you and you refuse to see it. Wake the fuck up!

Alright

I just saw it's after 1:00 AM here. Yikes. I better sign off soon. If you need me to buy your airline ticket on a card, send me a note later. Just will need to know the date you can fly, as it will be non-refundable, as well as your personal details. OK?

OK, I will see what I can do here, because I will still need money for my pocket, just in case. I am upset with myself right now.

Thanks for waking me up; it was a really 'enjoyable' call! You will have to keep me posted on your arrangements, sending me your flight details, etc. I love you.

Can you wire through Western Union or MoneyGram with your card online?

The shipment has made some movement. I think you can track it as well: molishippers.com tracking number 8890120474. It is showing 'In Transit Container Terminal 8 West'

Oh that is good!

I think it's at the container area now.

It will be moving out of the country soon! Thank God.

I thought it was going by air. Is it going by sea?

I have just Googled molishippers. They seem to be a shipping company, not a company that moves things by air. This is weird. Why would he have the gold sent by sea? That would take forever!

It's going to go by air. I paid for (an) air shipment.

K. Alright. I need to get to bed. It's going to be morning here all too soon.

Be safe! I love you!

Honey, I asked you a question.

Answer me before you leave.

Can you wire through Western Union or MoneyGram with your card online?

Or you can withdraw from the ATM, or cash advance on your credit card?

Gosh he is being so persistent. I'm really done with giving him money. If he lets me buy the ticket, I'll do it. But I'm not sending him any more money.

> I don't know about that. But I'm happy to just book your ticket.

Yes, I know. Please, honey. Understand me.

Alright go to sleep, I love you.

> Good night. Bye.

Believe it or not, I go onto Western Union to see if I can send Tom $5,000 for his flight. For some reason, probably God looking out for me, the system won't let me open an account. I'm so relieved. I didn't want to send it, but something made me try. I try MoneyGram as well, and it's rejected. At this point, I go to bed. I'll know soon enough if this is all real.

Day 26, January 27

Faith in Humankind

From: anniem@yahoo.com
Sent: Friday, January 27, 2017 1:52 PM
To: Tom Miller <happysmile4868@gmail.com>
Subject: Re: Reflection

Dearest Tom,

It's just about 2:00 in the afternoon here.

It's great to have the details of your business transaction complete! And I have reflected on the past week quite a bit. It was a real test for me. And it definitely was one of the longest weeks of my life! lol!

It tested my faith in humankind. It tested my generosity to help someone in need. It tested my trust in the universe. It tested my ability to have an open mind. It tested my dream for a different future. It tested my capability to believe in others. It tested my love for Tom Miller.

And I need to thank you, as God knows I didn't make it very easy for you (LOL. That's an understatement)! Thank you for your patience. Thank you for not walking away. Thank you for listening. Thank you for understanding how hard this was for me. Thank you for reassuring me with words, documents, and photos! Are you sure that is you in the HK photo? It kind of looks like a cut and paste job. I'm joking!!!!

Tom Miller, this was quite a test of our relationship. Never would I have imagined all of this back on Jan 2nd when you said hello on Match.

I am so looking forward to seeing you on Saturday! Your photos (which I printed; I'm old-fashioned that way) are here on my desk. I have been looking at them all day, smiling, dreaming, imagining, while working, of course! I just want to put 'the whole package' together: face, voice, smile, heart. Please come home soon!

So you'll read this when you wake. I should be finished working by then. Can't wait to catch up! My 'Hangouts' site is open and waiting for you.

You have captured my heart, soul, and mind, Tom. What an impact you have had on me. I am so happy you came into my life. Please do not leave!

I love you, Annie

I'm online ...

Hello, my love.

I have (a) problem with my cell phone.

I am very upset here and I am sorry for not getting back to you on time.

I love you so much and nothing can change that

I believe you are with Mum since I haven't heard from you.

I am home now ... if you see this and are online.

Hello, I am here.

What's going on?

Hey!!!!

What is going on with you? Why are you upset?

I am not upset

I am just not happy about myself.

I am sorry for coming into your life, Annie.

Why do you say that?

Because you think I am just asking you for help.
So you don't want to help me anymore. Which I
really need your help.

What is going on in HK that you are still there?
It must be more than just the ticket home.

Not sure if you are typing or lost the
connection ...

What in the world? Why is he still in HK? Why hasn't he flown home? Why is he mad at me?

No, it's not more than the ticket. I am waiting
for you to help me. I was trying to sell my
phone and laptop because you have turned
your back on me this time around.

Can you go to a Western Union office in HK?

Turned my back on him? What is talking about? I have sent him $15,000!!! This is just crazy.

My love, I can't go to Western Union in HK
because I go from the hotel and meet the
people then I come back to my hotel. I love and
respect you so much.

How can you say 'I have turned my back on you' when I have sent you a lot of money??? I haven't even lent a family member $15k!!!!

Honey, I didn't say that because of anything.

I am saying it because this is the time I need your support to get home.

And I have told you, we have a lot to talk about. You are so dear to me.

So are you ready for me to purchase your ticket?

Then you can be on your way!

Honey, I have told you to send the funds through Western Union and MoneyGram; you can do it online. Just 2k each on either site.

I went online today (aren't you shocked?) Western Union's site is not working. But I can go to one of their offices tomorrow, but you have to pick the money up at a Western Union office in HK. That is the only way to do it and have the money immediately. I am uncomfortable putting anyone else's name on the money or sending it to anyone else's account.

??

And if you 'argue' with me about this, it just makes me more uncomfortable. I am trying to help you.

One thing ... did you check the shipment online?

I haven't checked it yet.

It says it's on its way ... left Beijing. If the website is legitimate.

I appreciate everything you have done for me. I would never turn my back on you.

So, if the shipment is on its way, come home!!!!

I am grateful for you.

But help me understand. If the shipment is now flying from China to the US, why can't I buy you a ticket home?

What do you want to understand, tell me?

If the shipment is now in the air, coming to the US, why can't I buy you a ticket to come home today? If you leave at 3:00 pm your time, you'll arrive with the shipment.

Yeah, but I am telling you. With all respect. I want my agent to take care of my ticket for me. Just pick me up and let's go home.

You are stubborn!

Fuck the agent! He is crazy!

I am not stubborn(;) there are things he does on my booking. That makes me like it.

You need to understand me and let me arrive safe(ly) and pick me up.

If you are upset with me. I understand.

Oh, does this picture look like I am upset?

ha ha ha ha

So can you email your travel agent's details to me? Will he/she be picking up the money at a WU office? That is the only way to do it (the) same day. Otherwise it is three days (it says online).

BRB ... (I) need a drink.

LOL

You are funny. Why that?

Yes, Western Union is (the) same day. So how will you send the 4k?

I have never known anyone as giving as you. God bless you. I will make it up to you soon.

If you don't make it up to me, I will call an old boyfriend, who works for the government and tell him to FIND YOU! The only payment he will want is for me to say I'll marry him. Don't make me do that, please!!!

This is true ... and I will call the old boyfriend if I need to ...

You always go that extra mile to inspire and encourage me.

LOL

Nothing is going to happen. Stop thinking bad (sic) towards me because I know there are bad people out there. But I am not one of them.

I believe you, but you now know my connections and the consequences! Ha! So, I'll need the travel agent('s) name, probably phone number, maybe an address; not sure what else.

Western Union. You just need the name.

I think I sent money to Jack when he was in college. I needed (a) name and I thought (a) phone (number). I can see if it tells me online in the FAQs.

OK

Okay, it says the recipient must go to a Western Union office with (a) valid ID and the tracking number that I get. So who is he/she? I hope it is a he! Otherwise, I am VERY suspicious!

LOL You are funny.

She is married with three children and I don't even love her.

Suspicious?

What? It is a SHE??? You jerk! LOL

Me, a jerk?

YES YOU

ha ha ha

OK, what is this very ugly, fat and pimply travel agent's name?

LOL

Silly girl

All my insecurities will float away when you are here with me.

I guess I need her name and a way to contact her with the 'secret' code.

I will send it to her.

Yes, but I have to have her name when I go to the office.

Name : Emily Griffith

PHONE : 704-601-8363

How did you hook up with her?

We met at a business conference meeting.

So we became friends. And I have liked her ever since. She is honest and understanding. She books ticket(s) for a lot of stars in the country.

Her number is unlisted. I just did a Google search.

Gosh. So why do you always have to search on me(?)

It's Google! It's available!

Why? If you don't trust me, why are we here?

It's not about trust. It's just available, so I just use it. For work or whatever.

I have nothing to say to you.

I Google EVERYTHING. I'm like a millennial!

I am praying for the day we will be together.

Yes I understand you.

You hurt my feelings.

Please tell me.

I have nothing to say to you, quote, unquote

It hurt me too, that since we have stayed together and stuff.

So, if I send your agent the money, when do you plan to come home?

I will the same day

In case they ask, is the agent in NC? It's a 704 area code. I just don't want to be asked a question I can't answer and slow things down.

I have nothing left here to do.

Yes, yes they ask a lot of questions but just tell them to send it.

So what are your plans today?

indoors

Did you bring workout clothes?

How's the weather been?

BRB. Have to go to the washroom.

Sorry.

It's 0*C

In HK???? It should be much warmer than that!

Now that is weird. It should be really warm in Hong Kong. Oh gosh, my suspicions are on high alert again.

As for Hong Kong it's 18*C

Are you in Beijing or HK?

I am in HK.

Why do you ask?

I'm just confused. I asked above how the weather has been. And you replied it's 0*C.

Why

? BRB

I'm tired. I need to go to sleep.

OK, let's talk tomorrow. Good night from Pennsylvania.

We haven't resolved the flight issue. There is no way I am sending money to a travel agent. This is just crazy. And why would he say it's freezing in HK ...

Day 27, January 28

The Shipping Company

Good morning, my love.

Good evening to you. Do you know where your shipment is?

Honey, I haven't checked since last night.

But I will do right now.

Gosh, it's not even my shipment and I check at least three times a day ... ha

That is weird ... if I were shipping millions of dollars of anything, I'd be checking every second!!!

Ha because you care and I love you more than you can imagine.

Are you busy?

No ...

did you check the shipment?

Yes. Yes

Wow, it's already in the States.

Click on 'contact us.'

OK

Scroll down to the bottom for the address and phone number.

Yeah I can see it.

I was surprised to see a Newark NJ business address and a NC phone number.

Of course it's nothing. It's a one-man company.

You always have doubt, gosh. Curiosity kills a (sic) cat.

A one man freight forwarding company, really?

I am a very curious person when I have invested in something.

You should be too at $500k!

Yes I will pay you double with 10%.

Will this one-man operation call me before they deliver to my home, to ensure I am here?

Of course, they will call you.

Every deliver(y) person will call before coming to your door.

I do NOT want anything extra, not double, not interest. I just want back what I lent you.

OK, if you say so.

This is your business, your investment. I am only helping you out.

I adore you. I long to hold you close to me.

I have one other investigatory observation.

I long to be near to you.

And what is that?

Sorry to interrupt your beautiful, romantic words ...

When you ring both NC numbers, they have the 'exact' same recorded voicemail. Very strange.

What numbers?

The one for the shipper and the one for the travel agency.

It's the most bizarre thing. How can two totally different companies have the same message when you ring their number? And what a coincidence both have a NC prefix. Silly girl, don't you get it yet?

Strange...

Annie, so why all this (sic) things?

So is this how you are going to treat me, when we are together(?)

Then I won't ask you for (a) favor again.

Every time I question anything, he comes back with a threat.

I am 'invested,' so I do my homework. It has nothing to do with you directly.

Or, I should say it has nothing to do with how I feel about you. When I invest $15k, I take the time to understand the details. I am thorough. It's not about not trusting you.

I am a very detail-oriented person when it comes to business and finances.

Honey, sometimes there are some coincidences in life.

You can look alike, but it doesn't mean you are sisters or know each other from somewhere.

Yes, I am understanding it now. I thought you were referring to me.

No, not you!

I would never let you down. You have been so kind and caring and loving to me. And I will pay you back with my respect, love and to care for you forever when we are together.

What company did you hire to deliver the shipment to my house? You said you are using someone you trust.

Honey, they will call you, when coming (sic) I know nothing more. I just shipped it.

The papers give no details?

No, it didn't. It's the same company bringing it.

I am worried about you, and for you.

Yes, and that is why I have to leave.

Maybe you should stay there until the delivery arrives? In the event it doesn't come, you are there with the high court to do something about it.

I'm now being sarcastic. Somehow, I am reaching my limit with Tom. Oh, geez, isn't it about time?

Oh why do you say that?

If you don't want to meet me again, say it. Because why will (sic) you say such a thing?

I'm not saying that, silly! I am saying, maybe you should time your return once I confirm your investment has arrived.

OKOKOK, honey

What did you do for meals all day?

I had spaghetti. I like the spaghetti here.

Breakfast, lunch, and dinner?

Who has spaghetti when they go to Hong Kong?

LOL

No, my morning coffee always arrives.

And (for) lunch I take mango juice and a snack.

And in the evening I take any food, but not Hong Kong food.

I have a favor.

OK

Not sure how to phrase this.

What is that?

Please do not doubt my feelings for you.

In the priest's homily yesterday, he spoke of trust, which keeps coming up in our conversations.

He said we only trust the Lord by spending more time with him. And the same with our friends and others. So although you question my 'trust' of you, it is a function of needing more time with you. More time than 28 days. But know that even in these 28 days, you have captured my heart.

And that is my favor. To not doubt me.

I do not doubt my feelings for you.

I'm finished.

Thank you so much and I will make you happy.

Time will tell

Yes, time will tell.

I guess I have to get the heck out of bed, shower, and get my beautiful ass to West Chester.

It said online they are open till 5:00 ... I will call first.

Oh, OK, I see.

Do you want me to let you go now?

Please hold.

I just rang. We have an issue. You can't use a credit card when you go into a Western Union agent's office.

They only take debit or check, and as I told you, I'm tapped out.

Correction, not even a check; just cash or debit card.

Oh, so that means you have to send it online.

Yes, let me see if it is back in operation. It was down last night. I even called them. See, my thoroughness again! Ha

Ha

Their system is so f'ed up. It keeps thinking I want to send money to Australia!

Why is that? What's going on?

www.westernunion.com/us/en

Click on it.

I don't know. I put in that I am sending to the US and AUD come(s) up.

You have to change the country you are sending to. It's simple; I thought you were smart. LOL

HA HA HA!!!! AGAIN INTENTIONAL CAPS

https://secure.moneygram.com as for this, I believe you can even chat with them.

Hold on ...

Stay on the line. Just doing it now. I can now open an account which I couldn't do last night.

OK

Is Emily in the US?

Yes

Sorry for (the) delay. It is spinning/thinking. Not sure if going from that site to Hangouts caused the issue. Please hang on.

Oh, what issue is that?

Not letting my registration finalize. Will Emily be able to go to a WU location?

Of course, why do you ask?

Just going through their checklist. Stop being so suspicious and untrusting!!!

I need to get out of here.

Honey, I am feeling sleepy.

Ok, how do you want me to inform you or Emily? Sorry, the system seems to be slow. But I made progress. At least today I could open an account.

Yes, but why won't you try the MoneyGram? You can send online there as well.

Email me and I will wake up and email back or text me.

Can't send the same amount there. I checked last night.

I have to go to the washroom. Just give me a few mins.

But do what you have to do.

OK, go to sleep. I'll email you the results of my efforts. I love you, still new best friend, Tom Miller.

Okay, call when you are done.

I try to send money via Western Union, but the system won't let me set up an account. I call Tom to let him know. He's very annoyed and comments that he is not sure how he will get home. I suggest he contact his travel agent and ask them to invoice him for the ticket. I remind him that they should do this, given their long relationship. Since it's late in Hong Kong, we do not stay on the phone long. We agree to speak or IM the next morning.

Day 28, January 29

I Hate You

Phone call with Tom

Annie: Hi, Tom.

Tom: Hi, Annie, how are you?

Annie: Tom, did you look at the shipping company website?

Tom: Let me pull it up now ...

Annie: Tom, it says the shipment is held up in New York in customs. I called the shipping company and the guy was not very nice. He said there are additional fees. I told him that if he was a legitimate shipping company, that they would invoice you for the fees.

Tom: Why were you rude to them?

Annie: Tom, this is crazy. I have worked in the shipping business. No one ever asks for cash. This is all done with invoices and bills of lading.

Tom: I will call them now. I'll then get on Hangouts and give you an update.

Hello, honey.

I am here, honey.

Hey there. What did you find out?

Honey, I need you to help me get 45k.

For what?

For the document, of course.

If not, I will lose all my money to the States. Annie, please.

Did you leave me?

Sorry, the guy fixing my door was just leaving.

Tom, just have them invoice you for the work, as I said on the phone. That is how professional shippers do this.

And besides, I don't have $45k. I couldn't even give you $4000, remember?

Don't worry if you don't want to help me. It's not about an Invoice.

I understand.

It's your money, so if you tell me you won't help me, I will lose my (gold) bars to U.S. Customs. I understand.

Please don't turn this around to be my fault. First of all, the U.S. won't keep them. Secondly, you're a smart businessman, (so) tell them to bill you for the work they do for you. I worked in shipping in the past and never was money passed back and forth like this.

Now I'm fed up with Tom. It's taken this long for me to actually accept he is scamming me. Another $45,000 ... I don't think so ...

OK

Do the right thing. Get an invoice. Have a record of things and make your shipping company work FOR you. That is what you paid them for. And to think you criticized me for being 'rude' to them. Look how they are treating you!

So, you are not helping me or listening to me.

I know what I am talking about.

These things have to go through customs.

My best friend's dad works for customs ... I know it doesn't work this way ...

I need to get an anti-terrorism certificate

You can check it on Google.

I hate when you doubt me.

LOL

Your shipping company can do that too!!!

Seriously, anti-terrorism?

And the Kimberly certificate.

Yes, if they can do it, I have to pay them.

They told me they were going to do it by the time it gets here.

You just don't want to help me.

Thanks so much. You can go wherever you are going. You are always bringing friends into our relationship and talks.

Tom, you reached out to a woman who has many friends. I know people who work in customs, FBI, state police, etc. I'm well connected. I hope someday you return the $15k I lent you in good faith. You are right, we cannot have a relationship without trust. I'm sorry. You have all my contact info (I think I have yours ... I will know if what I sent to your home is returned). Again, any documents you need are the responsibility of the shipping company. As I said, if they are a legitimate company, they will send you a bill. Goodbye, my new best friend and lover, Tom. I pray that God keeps you in his care and looks after you. Be a good person. Return the $15k. Annie

What did you send to my house and who will be there to get it?

So you won't help me, thanks.

No, I cannot help you any more

That evening, at 1:00 AM, my phone rings. Tom Miller's name pops up. I don't answer it. He then rings again. I ignore the call a second time. Then he rings me a third time. I answer it.

Annie: Hello.

Tom: How are you?

Annie: I'm fine. What do you want?

Tom: Annie, won't you help me? I thought you trusted me? I have put all my savings into this business contract. I will lose everything. I promise to pay you back as soon as I get back to the States. I won't let you down. I swear.

Annie: Tom, I used to work for a shipping company. It doesn't work like this. If they need documents to get your shipment out of customs, they will create those documents for you and invoice you. That is what a shipping company does. You should not have to pay them anything in advance. If they are asking for money now, they are not reputable. Tom, be a good person. Do what is right. Pay me back what I lent you and stop this nonsense.

Tom: I hate you. I hate you.

He hangs up.

I'm shaken to the core. No one has ever told me they hated me ... and never with such anger. I lay in bed wondering if I have pushed Killer Miller too far. What will he do now? Will he send someone to my home? I clearly have upset him and made him really angry. I can't fall asleep for over an hour, totally frightened by his cold, harsh words.

The next day there are no texts, emails or messages from Killer Miller. But then later, in the middle of the night, my phone rings again. Curiosity makes me answer it. It's Killer Miller ...

Tom: Annie, hi.

Annie: Hello.

Tom: How are you?

Annie: How am I? I have never had anyone say they hate me ... let alone someone who, the day before, is telling me they love me.

Tom: I know. I called to say I'm sorry. I was angry.

Annie: Thank you for that. I appreciate it. Goodbye.

I hang up.

Day 29, January 30

My Last E-Mail

From: anniem@yahoo.com
Sent: Monday, January 30, 2017 9:08 AM
To: Tom Miller <happysmile4868@gmail.com>
Subject: Re: Good-bye

Tom:

Don't know if you will ever see this message. But I felt the need to say how disappointed I am that you were not the loving, honest person you pretended to be. In the dialogue above, you even swore on your mother's grave that you were being honest with me. I know I was stupid and gullible to have believed you. There were many signs that indicated you were lying to me. But I wanted to believe in the goodness of mankind. I wanted to trust you and believe you were a God-loving person. How can you live with yourself as a cheat and liar? How do you sleep at night? And how do you expect to ever find salvation when you are deceiving women? I feel sorry for you that you have to live this way. Your life must be very sad. You must need to cheat people to survive. How sad is that? Who are you really? Where do you live? Do you have a wife and a family? And what ever happened to the item I mailed to 'your house' ... Answers I am sure I will never have ...

The End

Epilogue

There were many red flags over the twenty-nine days Tom and I communicated. I noticed them throughout our phone and online conversations and rationalized nearly every one, except when the $45,000 request came through. I've listed all the inconsistencies on the pages that follow. You may have noticed even more!

I wanted to believe Tom was real. I let myself fall for him over the course of our one month connection. He was good at what he did; he drew me in.

After the $45,000 request, I called the FBI and tearfully revealed I had been scammed. They gave me the .com address for the Internet Corruption Agency (ICA) so I could file a report. I filed the report immediately, sharing every detail of phone numbers, email addresses, dating site names and login details, wire transfer details and the name and contact details for the shipping company. I did not hear back from the ICA. I hoped there was something they could do to find the people running this scam. I also rang the dating site to report Killer Miller. They assured me his profile would be blocked and deactivated.

Then, nearly five months later, I received a call from the Pennsylvania State Police. The detective introduced himself as Trooper V. He said a file had been sent to him from the FBI and he wanted to investigate my incident. If I was willing, he would like me to meet him at the state police office to be interviewed.

I could not believe my case would be investigated. I was so excited! I agreed to meet with Trooper V and we spent over two hours going over the events, email addresses, phone numbers, and Hangouts dialogue. I was embarrassed to share the details, but he reassured me that this type of scam happened more often than I could imagine. I felt more at ease telling him the story.

I asked Trooper V why he was taking the time to investigate a case that only amounted to $15,000 in fraud. He said that the state police were responsible for the safety of the people in my community, and it was his duty to follow up. How about that?!

Over the next six months, Trooper V conducted a full investigation. He researched the credit card used to purchase the flowers that were sent to my work office. He traced the phone numbers to identify the identity and location of the callers. He involved the U.S. Homeland Security Department and the Federal Reserve to track the wire transfers. He also contacted the Hong Kong Police to report the incident.

And remember the Valentine's Day card I mailed to Tom Miller in Pittsburgh? Well, Trooper V also sent a state trooper to that address to see if anyone recalled receiving mail from me. A gentleman named Tom Miller answered the door that day. The state trooper explained the purpose of his visit. This 'Tom Miller' (whose identity had been stolen) was so happy to hear from the state police. Tom had received my Valentine, and evidently it had caused quite an issue with his wife, Rebecca, who presumed her husband was having an affair. She wanted to know who Annie was and why she was sending her husband a Valentine's Day card. You can imagine Tom and his wife's relief to learn the real story.

I found out that HONGKONG TRADING COMPANY LTD was a shell company without assets. The false Tom Miller was probably someone who lived in Europe or Africa. There was no way to find him. A police inspector in Hong Kong contacted me by email and said I had until the end of the year to file a legal claim against the trading company. The dollars that I had wired to the trading company would be frozen in the account until year's end.

I am a pretty driven person, and I knew I had been scammed. I decided to learn what would be involved in filing a lawsuit in Hong Kong. I contacted a U.S. lawyer I knew and asked if he had any contacts in Hong Kong. I was given the name and number for a corporate law firm in Hong Kong. They said my case was too small for them, but referred me to another firm and a Mr. Lee, who was a reputable Hong Kong attorney. I was making progress!

Mr. Lee sent me a long message explaining the Hong Kong legal system, which follows:

Dear Ms. St. Clair,

I have quickly read the documents you provided. If I understand it correctly, you have earlier remitted a total sum of USD 15,000 to the bank account of a company called Hong Kong Trading Co. Ltd with the International Bank of Hong Kong. The remittance was made as a result of fraudulent representation to you by one Thomas Miller. You intend to claim back the money. The money is now remaining in the International Bank of Hong Kong account, which has been frozen by the Hong Kong police. If my understanding is wrong, please let me know.

Subject to obtaining further information and instructions and having a more thorough consideration of the case, my preliminary observation is that you may need to sue Hong Kong Trading Co. Ltd (the holder of the account and recipient of the fund) and/or Thomas Miller (the perpetrator of the fraud). Since the amount involved is only USD 15,000, which is roughly equivalent to HKD 117,000, it is important you first consider the possible costs implications of a legal claim in Hong Kong.

The amount of money claimed falls within the jurisdiction of the District Court of Hong Kong (which is the 2nd tier of the civil courts of first instance of Hong Kong below the High Court). In Hong Kong, civil litigation lawyers normally charge on time spent. My current hourly rate for District Court cases is HKD 4,000. The first step is to prepare and issue a writ (a sort of claim form) with a detailed statement of claim. The writ will be served on the defendant(s). If the defendant(s) intends to defend, the defendant(s) must give notice of intention to defend within a specified period. Thereafter, the defendant(s) must file and serve a defense within another specified period. The action will then go on stage by stage (e.g., mutual discovery of documents, exchange of witness(es) statements etc.) all the way until trial. It will usually take one to two years for the action to reach the trial, and sometimes it can be even longer. Of course, it is possible that the action may end earlier through settlement at any stage of the proceedings. On the other hand, if the defendant(s) does/do not even give notice of intention to defend or file a defense within the specified period, you will be entitled to apply for default judgment against the defendant(s) without going through the process to trial. It is therefore difficult at this stage to give a realistic estimate of the legal costs to be incurred for obtaining a judgment because it will depend on whether the defendant(s) will be defending vigorously and at what stage the action will end. Just as a very rough estimate, the legal costs to be incurred all the way up to trial may be around HKD 300,000 to HKD 500,000 or even more. It may, therefore, far exceed the amount claimed.

If the defendant(s) does/do not defend, the estimated costs for obtaining a default judgment will be much cheaper by about HKD 10,000 to HKD 20,000. However, I note that Thomas Miller is unlikely to be a Hong Kong resident. After the writ is issued, there must be application to the court for permission to serve the writ outside the jurisdiction of Hong Kong. This will result in additional costs of about HKD 10,000 plus the legal costs of a U.S. attorney effecting service in the U.S. and making an affidavit to confirm service. At present, I am not sure whether Hong Kong Trading Co. Ltd is a Hong Kong company. If it is incorporated overseas, similar steps will have to be followed in that country. There is one more thing you need to consider. Legal action once commenced cannot be stopped or withdrawn unless there is a settlement or unless the court permits (which is usually conditional upon you paying the legal costs of the defendant(s). So if the defendant(s) really defends the action, you cannot unilaterally stop and must continue with the action. In addition, obtaining a judgment (whether default judgment or judgment after a trial) is not the end of the matter. If the defendant(s) do/does not pay, enforcement action will have to be taken. In this case, one possibility is to apply for a garnishee order to order the International Bank of Hong Kong to pay the money in the bank account to you. Application of a garnishee order will incur additional costs, estimated to be about HKD 20,000 to HKD 30,000. In this regard, I do not know how long the police will be able to freeze the money. To avoid the risk of the police ceasing to freeze the money in the interim period, a possible step is to apply for an interlocutory injunction. However, an application for an interlocutory injunction is very expensive and the costs of such an application alone can easily exceed HKD 100,000. This may be too high as compared with the amount claimed and you may not opt for it despite the possible risk of the police ceasing to freeze the money.

If you win, normally you will be entitled to be compensated by the defendant(s) for the costs you incurred. But even if you are awarded costs, whether or not you are able to recover such costs from the defendant(s) is uncertain. It is most unlikely that Thomas Miller is a Hong Kong resident or has any asset in Hong Kong. If he is a fraudster, it is unlikely you will be able to find him or his asset, whether in Hong Kong or elsewhere in the world. Hong Kong Trading Co Ltd appears to be a limited company with limited liability. We do not know whether it has any asset. If it is a company set up or controlled by Thomas Miller for doing fraudulent acts, it is most unlikely that it will have any asset. So there is a real risk that even if you win and obtain a costs order against them, it will be an empty judgment/order.

So the above are the risks or implications of legal costs which are independent from the merit of your claim, and which you must consider before bringing legal action here. Even if you are able to get back the USD 15,000, you may not be able to get back the legal costs you spent depending on whether Thomas Miller or Hong Kong Trading Co Ltd has assets. Lastly, there is one more matter which you may need to know. If Thomas Miller or Hong Kong Trading Co Ltd decide to defend the legal action and they want to put you off, they may apply for an order requiring you to pay a sum of money into the court as security for their costs on the grounds you are not a Hong Kong resident, and if they win, they may be able to recover from you their legal costs of the action. Unfortunately, under Hong Kong law, security for costs only applies to a non-Hong Kong plaintiff and not to a non-Hong Kong defendant(s). The rationale behind this is that a plaintiff suing somebody is a deliberate choice, while a defendant who is sued is passive. So, only a non-Hong Kong plaintiff may be required to give security for costs, but not a non-Hong Kong defendant.

I hope the above provide(s) you with some idea about legal action in Hong Kong. If you decide to sue and need my services, I will discuss with you further on the way forward.

Regards,
Mr. Lee
Solicitor
Hong Kong

Mr. Lee tried to convince me not to move forward with the suit, as it could end up costing me hundreds of thousands of dollars in legal fees if the defendant decided to drag it on and on. I was convinced that would not happen. I instructed Mr. Lee to start the process, which was to issue a 'Demand Letter' that essentially gave the defendant ten days to return the money to me or a legal proceeding would be commenced.

The ten days came and went. This meant I had a decision to make. Did I now move forward with the formal legal proceeding or drop the whole thing? I decided to move forward. Something told me that the trading company would not let this go to court.

My attorney issued a writ, which was served to the director of the Trading Company. The defendant would then have 14 days to give notice of his intent to defend the suit. If he gave notice, he then had another 28 days to file and serve a defense. If the defendant did not file and serve a defense, then we could apply for a default judgement to be entered, which would enable me to get back the money without a formal lawsuit.

Waiting for the next 14 days was excruciating. Whenever I questioned if I had done the right thing, I went back to the fact I had been wronged and there was no way this would go to court. On day 13, Mr. Lee contacted me and said a Chinese man and woman came into his office with a check for $16,600. Mr. Lee told them the amount was $17,000 to cover the money his client sent, plus interest, plus attorney's fees. The couple then took another $400 in cash out of their wallet and handed it to Mr. Lee.

Once the check had cleared, Mr. Lee wire transferred the money to me. I had won!

Why did I write *19 Days*? Some asked me if I did this for therapy. I must say, I was quite upset with myself for being so gullible and being conned. I had truly fallen for this guy in just nineteen days. I cried a lot and replayed the twenty-nine total days over and over in my mind, asking myself why I had continued the dialogue with Killer Miller. I thought I wouldn't ever go on another dating site again, telling myself, *See, you shouldn't have signed up for that stupid site.*

But that is not why I wrote this book. I wrote it for all the women who are involved in internet dating or considering it. I'm sharing my story so you can understand firsthand how easy it is to get drawn in and to fall in love, even when you haven't met your perfect match in person. I hope this story helps other women to report abuse and scams or recognize when it's happening before it's too late. And I hope it helps law enforcement find these horrible people who prey on innocent women.

I've also learned that men can be scammed as easily as women. Male friends of mine have spoken of the very young, beautiful women who 'wink' at them. Women much younger than themselves make these men feel handsome, attractive, sexy, and wanted. The scams work in a similar way, ultimately asking for money. Some figure it out before paying a penny; others do not.

And, of course, the dating site I joined had warning messages: don't speak to someone on your personal email, don't provide personal information about yourself (date of birth, address, mother's maiden name, etc.), don't send them money, and make sure you meet them in a public place when you meet the first few times. Did I read the warnings? Yes. Did I heed them? Not until it was too late.

Happy dating, but please be careful, and listen to those tiny voices in your head telling you it just can't be real. And please share your stories on my blog at 19DaysBook.com so we can all educate each other.

Red flags I noticed.

Perhaps you picked up others …

1. We moved to Google Hangouts straight away at his suggestion, moving us from the Match platform, which dating apps warn against.

2. We did not speak on the phone till day seven, perhaps to avoid making a personal connection. And when we did speak, his voice did not match how I thought he would sound, given his photos.

3. He didn't remember I had a son after I sent a long email about myself, nor did he remember my daughter was stillborn, suggesting he wasn't really engaged in the conversation, regardless of how personal it had seemed.

4. At times his answers seemed rehearsed or prepared, as if he was speaking from a script.

5. He first said he was born in Lisbon and later said he was born in NYC, indicating discrepancies about himself, which I did not notice at the time.

6. His English in Hangouts was not very good, yet the alleged 'erotic dream' was in nearly perfect English, suggesting it was copied from somewhere.

7. He indicated on his Match profile that he was divorced, yet later he said

his wife passed away. When I questioned it, he described her passing as too painful, so that I would not press him further.

8. He asked for iTunes cards twice; were these small requests just softening me up for the big financial asks?

9. Tom did not realize he had a layover in DC on his way to Hong Kong, meaning the trip was fake.

10. He said he could walk to the DC airport from downtown, which also indicated he was nowhere near the airport in DC or didn't know the layout of the city.

11. He said the airline called to check on him, which just doesn't happen in today's world, even if you are flying first class.

12. It should have taken longer to fly to Asia from the US, again an indication the trip was not real.

13. He said it took two hours to drive from Beijing to Hong Kong; I presumed he meant to fly to Hong Kong, but even that is too short of a time frame.

14. He asked for $7,000 and didn't want his name on the wire transfer, nor did he want me to tell anyone about the transfer. He knew my friends and family would question what I was doing and talk me out of it.

15. The little voice in my head told me not to make the payments, but I did not listen, as I wanted to believe in him.

16. He forgot the time zone difference, saying good morning to me when I had just had my day, which indicated he really wasn't in Asia.

17. He got defensive whenever I questioned him or an inconsistency, using emotional blackmail to manipulate me.

18. Even if his bank account had been frozen, he should have been able to get a flight back to the US with the support of his travel agent; just another indication that the trip was a fake.

19. I seemed to be checking the status of the shipment more than Tom was, which wouldn't be the case when an individual is making a significant financial investment for their business.

20. He said it was zero degrees in Hong Kong when it should be warm in January, indicating he wasn't actually in Hong Kong.

21. He referred to his travel agent as he and then gave me a woman's name, showing that he wasn't keeping his own story straight.

22. He would change the subject when I asked too many questions about him or the business transaction to distract me from uncovering more untruths.

About the Author

Photograph by Mark Aizenberg Photography

A native of Philadelphia, Pennsylvania, Anne St. Clair spent a number of years living overseas in Melbourne, Australia and Brussels, Belgium while working for a global petrochemical company. After repatriating to the United States, Anne continued her rewarding career by joining a professional services firm and serving the Higher Education and Healthcare industries.

Anne has an amazing and inspiring centenarian mother, an adult son of whom she is very proud, and is in a supportive and committed relationship.

Anne believes in love, romance, and second chances. She knows how hard it is to meet someone when you are single and over fifty. She also understands that internet dating can be scary and requires a person to be comfortable with being vulnerable in a digital world.

Anne wrote this story to share the potential risks of internet dating. She wants readers to recognize the schemes and tactics that are used to manipulate and ultimately deceive. With this knowledge, other men and women will be more equipped to not just notice, but also heed, any red flags in emails, chats and conversations.

In addition, Anne experienced the regret and embarrassment of being deceived by another human being. It took courage to speak about these events with family, friends, the police and international authorities. Anne hopes this book encourages others to not be afraid. To share when they have been wronged. To trust that goodness will prevail over evil.